GAYS AND FILM

Edited by Richard Dyer

REVISED EDITION

New York Zoetrope

GAYS & FILM

Library of Congress Cataloging in Publication Number: 84-061788

ISBN   0-918432-58-8

New York Zoetrope
80 East 11th Street
New York 10003
Printed in the United States of America
First Printing, revised edition: October 1984

Introduction

No social group can afford to ignore the importance of the cinema. Although perhaps eclipsed today by television, it has been for most of the century the mode of communication, expression and entertainment—the 'signifying practice'—*par excellence*. It has acted as a repository of images of how people are and how they should be, images that are both produced by and help to produce the general thought and feeling of our culture. In addition, it is widely regarded, for good or ill, as a peculiarly 'rich' medium, involving as it does so many different elements (spectacle, narrative, performance, photography, music, speech, montage, movement etc.) and, in most cases, so many people. This 'richness' gives cinema its status, as 'complex art' and as marvellous, grand-scale entertainment.

It also makes it a useful subject of study, for the richness of the elements constitutes a mass of contradictions that are, with varying degrees of success, marshalled into coherent, rounded-off 'wholes'. Study can expose these contradictions and the processes by which they are masked, and in so doing expose the ideological contradictions and con-tricks of our society.

As an inescapable shaper and reflector of thought and feeling, as a prestigious form of art and entertainment, as a particularly useful subject of study, cinema is important for gay people as for any other social group. In addition, as Caroline Sheldon and Jack Babuscio make clear in their essays, gays have had a special relationship with the cinema, for several reasons. Because, as gays, we grew up isolated not only from our heterosexual peers but also from each other, we turned to the mass media for information and ideas about ourselves. Until recently, films have been just about the only widely accessible source of such ideas, and we have had, unfortunately, to rely on them a good deal. (Even with the coming of television this has remained largely true, since until very recently indeed, gayness was still a taboo subject for 'family viewing'.) This isolation (and the feelings of self-hate that much of the imagery we learnt in the cinema instilled in us) perhaps also made the need to escape more keen for us than for some other social groups—so, once again, we went to the pictures. Once there, however, we could use the films— especially those *not* directly offering us images of ourselves—as we chose. We could practise on movie images what Claude Lévi-Strauss has termed '*bricolage*',[1] that is, playing around with the elements available to us in such a way as to bend their meanings to our own purposes. We could pilfer from straight society's images on the screen such that would help us build up a sub-

1

culture, or what Jack Babuscio calls a 'gay sensibility'. Finally, one of the things you learn fastest if you are gay is the ability to pass for straight, to perform, to make illusions. Equally, one of the predominant concerns of twentieth-century drama has been human behaviour seen in terms of role-playing, theatricality, performance, illusion etc.[2] The cinema—the most widely available drama before television—offered us, unconsciously no doubt (for it as well as for us), an endless examination of this vital aspect of our everyday lives.

Given the importance of the cinema for gay people (even for those who do not share the special involvement with the cinema sketched in the previous paragraph), what questions should we pose of it? Caroline Sheldon, in her essay, suggests four, which are, to varying extents, reflected in the rest of this pamphlet.

First, there is the question of pornography. Apart from Caroline's own discussion of it, this question is not directly tackled elsewhere in the pamphlet. In particular, the issue of the definition of pornography and whether or not it is defensible or valuable has not been tackled. This is partly because one cannot tackle everything, but mainly because the debate about pornography seems so hopelessly enmeshed in moral posturing (on both sides) that any useful intervention in it needs to be concerned principally with changing the terms of the debate. The question of pornography is important for gay politics — one of the solutions that this society is capable of offering to gay oppression is 'permissiveness', including pornography. The relation of permissiveness to liberation (two versions of freedom) is, however, deeply problematic, and urgently needs exploration.[3]

The question of pornography does arise in the pamphlet indirectly in connection with the filmography. Lesbianism is a commonplace in porno-graphy for heterosexual men, and there has been a considerable increase in male gay pornography in recent years. As a result, the filmography shows a preponderance of obviously pornographic titles. In compiling the filmography, I did wonder whether I should exclude pornography, but I realised that I could not. It is significant that gayness should have emerged most prolifically in that area, and the fact that it has needs to be registered. Equally I am not persuaded that *The Devil in Miss Jones* is more degrading than *The Killing of Sister George,* or that *Boys in the Sand* is less worthwhile than *Boys in the Band.* To have omitted pornography would have been to capitulate both to the questionable distinction between pornography and non-pornography, and to acknowledge the 'superiority' of the latter. However, inclusion of porno-graphy in the filmography should not be taken as indicating any easy endorsement of it in terms of some notion of 'sexual freedom'.

Caroline's second area of work is stereotyping. This is an area that has always attracted our anger and yet, as I found out when trying to write my essay, one that is relatively little explored in any systematic way and full of contradictions and confusions. Yet it remains an important area, for it is from representations of social groups that people get their 'knowledge' about those groups — and that goes for members of those groups themselves.

2

The third area in Caroline's essay — films that are generally known to be of interest to lesbians — relates to Jack Babuscio's essay on camp and the gay sensibility, and indeed to Noel Purdon's recent observation that

It must be clear that what we understand by gay cinema cannot merely be the same as the depiction of gays in films. It includes the whole creative process and working relationship experienced by a gay mentality employed in the cinema.[4]

As Caroline and Jack both indicate, this expression of gayness through non-gay representations is an important strategy of subversion for gays in relation to the cinema. This subversion may be in the films and/or in our response to them; the gay sensibility or mentality may be at work at the point of production ('encoding') and/or at the point of consumption ('decoding'). Either way it goes against the grain of the film and the culture—hence the feeling that many people have (including Noel Purdon) that camp is trying to 'drag things down'. That is just what it is trying to do.

Finally, Caroline deals with films made by, for and about gay women. The area of gay production is, of course, although not dealt with directly outside her essay, implicit in the whole pamphlet. In discussing the possibility of a radical use of typing (the final sections of Caroline's essay and mine), or in defending the procedures of the gay sensibility in relation to film (Caroline's third section, and the whole of Jack's essay), or, more generally, in exploring the relation between our different positions on gay politics and films, we are all concerned centrally and crucially with the question of what a truly gay film would be like. In this perspective, the films of Barbara Hammer and Jan Oxenburg and the British independent feature film in progress, *Nighthawks* (which are scheduled for the NFT season), are of particular interest.

As mentioned above, the political positions of Caroline, Jack and myself are quite clearly different in many ways, and this reflects three of the main differences of emphasis and direction within the gay movement. Equally, there are many points of overlap between the three essays. I hope this means that we are genuinely in dialogue with each other, and that the essays will, taken together, be useful in stimulating dialogue within the gay movement. Equally the issues raised are quite clearly part of current debates in film criticism and study on questions of ideology and sexuality, the possibilities of subversion and the problems of building a revolutionary practice of film making and film viewing.

Many people have, often unwittingly, contributed to this booklet. For ideas and help, my thanks to, among others, Ken Bartlett, Charlotte Brunsdon, Bob Cant, Colin Cruise, Gillian Hartnoll, Sylvia Harvey and Hilary Thompson, the staff of the BFI Information and Documentation Department, Brian Baxter of the NFT for help with the season, and Nicky North and David Meeker for help with film viewings. Finally may I thank especially my two co-contributors, Caroline Sheldon and Jack Babuscio, for the amount of work they put in, in Caroline's case at very short notice, and Angie Martin for

3

doing far more, intellectually and practically, than the mere title 'editor' conveys.

Richard Dyer

Notes

1. Claude Lévi-Strauss, *Totemism*, Penguin, 1969.
2. See Elizabeth Burns, *Theatricality*, Longman, London 1972.
3. For an initial opening up of the problem of 'permissiveness', see 'Within these Walls', *Gay Left* No. 2.
4. Noel Purdon, 'Gay Cinema', *Cinema Papers*, (Melbourne), No. 10, Sept-Oct 1976, p. 116.

Postscript (1980)

Since *Gays and Film* came out, some discussions of homosexuality have cast into doubt the validity of producing such a book. Broadly, these discussions centre on the very category 'homosexual' itself. Work by, for example, Foucault, McIntosh and Weeks[1] argues persuasively that while homosexual activity is universal, the category of persons called 'homosexuals' is of relatively recent date in this culture. In this perspective, work which addresses itself to this category seems to be accepting a purely historical division of sexuality into hard and fast categories which cut across the fluidity of human sexuality.

However, because a category is historically and socially constructed, it is not any less real. (All social constructions limit humanity, but they are also the only means by which we can be human at all.) 'Homosexual' is an historical category by which people really live. Gay work has to analyse this category and cannot operate as if it were already dissolved by political struggle. Moreover, the category has to be defended because of the fact of oppression. In terms of the politics of representation, fighting oppression is particularly difficult for gays because we are 'invisible'. The problem of identification with others as a basis for action (to defend and transform sexual practices) is then particularly acute and leads to the troublesome conclusion – in my article here – that some form of *recognisable* representational form is a political necessity for gay people.

Notes

1. Michel Foucault, *A History of Sexuality*, Allen Lane, London, 1979; Mary McIntosh, 'The Homosexual Role', *Social Problems*, vol. 16, no. 2, Fall 1968; Jeffrey Weeks, *Coming Out*, Quartet, London, 1977.

4

Lesbians and film: some thoughts

by Caroline Sheldon

The average gay woman goes to the cinema as much as everyone else, and like the bulk of the cinema public is hardly catered for in terms of her own reality. Films in general distribution tend to emphasise either middle-class life styles (lesbians are not necessarily middle-class) or escapist male heroics of a kind unavailable to the public. Unfortunately when lesbians do appear the effect is far more negative than their simple absence. Lesbianism is usually shown as an aberration, an individual psycho-social problem, which may not be the condition of every lesbian in the audience but may help to precipitate a few into believing that it is. This analysis in itself could become a psycho-social one — which could be useful for those still doubting that dominant ideologies have any effect in the make-up of a particular class, caste or group's expectations.

As commodities (determined by the profit motive in production and distribution) and as ideological products (determined by a multitude of historical, social and cultural factors), films are often tools to maintain depoliticisation. At the same time, they may give clues as to the mode of operation of capitalist/patriarchal power. Given the political perspective of lesbianfeminism, a term which I shall clarify, I shall be discussing quite a large number of films, made by men and women, which reflect on the position of lesbians in society. Out of this political stance, a number of distinct areas appear as needing analysis and I shall be indicating some possibilities of approach to a) pornographic and *avant-garde* cinema and homosexuality; b) stereotyping of lesbians in contemporary film; c) films of interest to lesbians; d) women's films and lesbians' films.

The politics of lesbianfeminism

The colour of my gayness is red and white, the colour of my feminism is lavender. *The author*

Lesbianfeminism implies a certain analysis of the power structure in which sexism is the primary oppression and lesbianism is defined as a political and emotional choice.

The analysis of the development of capitalism as undertaken by Engels[1] points to the institutionalisation of the family, with its division of labour according to gender, as basic to the establishment of private property and

5

class differentiation. The only way men could be sure of transmitting their property to their own children was by owning the women who bore their sons (etymologically, *'pater'* derives from power and *'familias'* from slaves). It is this pattern of dominance, whose form has changed somewhat over the centuries, though remaining one where men have the power, which is termed the patriarchy.

Modern capitalism depends on the heterosexual family unit to produce workers already alienated by the experience of lack of power (in childhood) and by a strictly defined sexuality. For exploited men, the power of men over women and children substitutes for control over their own fates. Traditionally homosexuality operates in this system as *the criminal element* — both as a warning to those stepping out of line and a method of containment of anti-social (anti-heterosexual) tendencies.

The idea of lesbianism is used to maintain non-association and rivalry between women: the husband and children must remain the priority in a woman's life. In this light, the lesbian can be described as *that potential part of every woman which capitalist patriarchal society represses.* This definition finds support from a surprising quarter in the Freudian theory of development which shows the girl-child torn from her primary love-object (mother) to be forced to adjust to a secondary love-object (father). [2] In this Freud saw women as inherently more bisexual than men. [3] The re-orientation of the girl-child's developing sexuality can only be effected by instilling a particularly deep sense of powerlessness and self-hate (unparalleled in the development of the male child), necessitating the later choice of a powerful love-object, to be identified with and protected by. Hand in hand with these 'benefits' of heterosexuality are those of social status, economic survival, physical protection ('Gallantry is the system of dominance in which men protect women from other men' [4]) and being a 'real woman'.

In the context of Freudian analysis lesbianism is viewed either as an arrested stage of development or as regression since the woman takes her mother as primary love-object model, rather than her father. Furthermore, it is also viewed, logically, as (role) identification with the father. This implication of value-judgement is fully borne out both by society and many therapists in the definition of lesbianism as sickness.

The analysis of women's common oppression, especially during the past century, has begun to break down the divisions between women that patriarchal society fostered, and there is an increasing sense of woman-identification — pride in being a woman and a self-confidence based on a genuine and growing sense of powerfulness and identity. In this analysis lesbianism emerges as a key issue, as society tries to ostracise and diffuse the Women's Movement by describing it as being made up of lesbians and man-haters. As Ti-Grace Atkinson has written:

Lesbianism for feminism is not 'another' issue or 'another' example of human oppression. Nor is lesbianism about 'autonomy'. Lesbianism is pretty clearly about 'association' — not about aloneness. If lesbianism were

6

about aloneness, it could hardly be relevant to anything in the political sense.[5]

Given the enormous amount of sexism inherent in heterosexual relationships and an assumed potential bisexuality, the question is raised as to why so many 'liberated' women continue to cling to heterosexual privileges (status, protection, etc.) and fear to commit themselves to other women on the basis of real love, solidarity and association. And to quote Ti-Grace Atkinson again:

There are women in the Movement who engage in sexual relations with other women, but who are married to men; these women are not lesbians in the political sense. These women claim a right to private lives; they are collaborators.
There are other women who have never had sexual relations with other women, but who have made and live a total commitment to this Movement. These women are lesbians in the political sense.[6]

What is being questioned is not so much sexuality, it is *male-identification* (identification with the male-definition of the world, with men's needs, desires and cultural hegemony). Male-identification can be seen as operating in the Freudian archetype of the weak, self-hating woman, the lesbian who must play a male role (and the woman for whom revenge against men is the organising principle of her life) since their self-definition is based, in one way or another, on their relationship to man's 'natural' position of power. Lesbianfeminists describe themselves as *'woman-identified'* (identification in solidarity with women's struggles for an autonomous identity, social position and new consciousness).

It seems then that separatism is inherent to a lesbianfeminist analysis (though in practice there is a possibility of forming alliances with men on the basis of allied and shared oppressions — class, race, etc. — but never at the cost of compromising the struggle against sexism and heterosexism).

Role-playing is criticised by lesbianfeminists in its assumption of power-based heterosexual models. Taking on oppressing or oppressed role-models is no way to change the balance of power. At the same time much is to be learnt from the oppression of lesbians and their way of dealing with it; and the real emotional commitment to other women, in the context of its social unacceptability, demands respect.

The taboo on lesbianism means that historically and culturally there is more or less silence about the ways in which lesbians are oppressed, though this seems to have varied considerably in relation to the oppression of all women. Furthermore, the fact that lesbians come from all kinds of class and racial backgrounds, as well as having very different statuses in society, makes the lesbianfeminist debate a microcosm of discussion and action on the linked oppressions under patriarchal capitalist society.[7] A crucial part of this debate is the power of the media and the roles it assigns to lesbian women. My discussion of film takes place in this context.

The criminal element: male and female homosexuality in pornographic and *avant-garde* film

Who wants to know about queers anyway?

The financial interests of the cinema as (voyeuristic) entertainment have led to the exploitation of the criminal, mainly evidenced by the large numbers of outlaw, gangster, murder, detective and police films designed for mass-consumption, which have been constantly produced throughout the history of film. No other criminal element in society has been as proportionally unrepresented in such films as the homosexual (sadists have a greater audience). The unacceptability of the homosexual theme in the 1950s, for example, is illustrated by the fact that Clouzot's *Les diaboliques* (1954), a complex mystery story in which a husband and his mistress conspire to get rid of his wife was based on Boileau and Narcejac's *La femme qui était* in which the conspirators are a lesbian couple.

The criminality of homosexuality correlates with its greater visibility in films only partially available to the general public: the *avant-garde* and hard porn, whose semi-illegal status puts them, like the homosexual, safely 'underground' or out of the way of respectable society.* In this area however sex difference operates: the *avant-garde* has largely been concerned with male homosexuality, and porn with lesbianism. This isn't to say that there is no gay male porn, but what there is has been exclusively geared to a male homosexual audience. A certain lesbian *avant-garde* is in the making, but it is a recent and little known phenomenon (see below, p. 19 for a discussion of this) and bears more relation to the emergence of lesbianfeminism than to the 'traditions' of the *avant-garde*. This sex difference in the representation of homosexuality is one that surprises no-one, in the same way that many of the inherent sexisms of patriarchal culture were considered 'natural' before they were exposed and analysed.

Both male and female homosexuals are defined by the patriarchy primarily in terms of their sexuality, and women in general are defined by their sex role. Heterosexual men escape this system by being primarily defined by their activity in society at large, *i.e.* by their work, though under capitalism other terms denoting inferiority are often used, such as of race or class (also additionally applied to homosexuals and women). This is in agreement with homosexuals and women being defined in relation to men: this relationship is basically one of sex-object to subject. In this lies the key to the discussion of the preponderance of first, lesbians in pornography and second, male gays in the *avant-garde*.

*Here the comparison is not only between the criminality of homosexuality and these films (their liability to prosecution on the grounds of obscenity) but also the measure to which they are outlawed—*i.e.* seen as outside society and the law (unprotected by it). Obviously there are wider implications than are indicated here, but these are beyond the scope of this monograph.

8

The double-definition of lesbian sexuality (as a woman, she 'should' be available to a man, and yet is one who makes love with other women) makes her a heavily charged sex-symbol in a society where men (and women) often know little or nothing about women's sexuality (the myth that operates here is 'lesbians are fantastic in bed'). The mysterious (and possibly threatening/castrating) nature of women's sexuality is made safe in the porno flick by the distance between the onlooker and the screen.[8] Lesbianism is therefore an ideal theme for the porn market. Furthermore, men can only experience lesbian love-making voyeuristically (not true of male homosexuality) and can do so under the guise of 'education', a common rationalisation encouraged by all pornography. The ever-present question of 'How do they do it?' is being answered in a way that makes the onlooker feel that he can take on the technical knowledge (and thus the power) of the lesbian.

The theme of lesbianism is further made safe by the usual arrival at some point in the action of a man who satisfies the 'real cravings' of the women, and allows *full* identification to the onlooker, so the initial lesbian love-making is being put fully at the service of heterosexuality: the familiar myth that 'all a lesbian needs is a good screw' — and the speaker is the right man for the job. The depersonalisation of this language reflects the film language of porno flicks.

The theme of lesbianism at the service of heterosexuality appears in the soft porn film *Emmanuelle* in a slightly more sophisticated form. The audience is invited to view the sexual education of the young heroine, who arrives at her husband's beautiful villa in Thailand as a healthy and promiscuous heterosexual (the same old strategy of 'education' in a form which gives the viewer the option of identifying either with the educator or the educated). She soon graduates from masturbating in the company of a young girl friend to being seduced by a slightly older woman on the squash courts, and to falling in love and running away with the mysterious Bee, an archaeologist. Unfortunately Bee leaves her and she returns to her husband to have her sexual education completed by an old roué, who will initiate her into the joys of masochism. The message of the film is clear: the homosexual interlude was a stage she had to get through before getting to the 'real thing': total passivity.

Voyeuristic treatment of lesbianism is not limited to pornography, it often surfaces in conventional film, as we shall see later. In a strategy dear to the cinema, John Huston's *The Kremlin Letter* uses double-voyeurism*: the audience watch the spies watching the seduction of a Russian diplomat's daughter by a black lesbian (the sequence is completely overloaded with sexual symbolism with the added touch of the woman's race). In this case lesbianism is being put not only at the service of heterosexuality (eventually helping to introduce the hero to the woman of his dreams), but also at the service of the political defence of capitalism, as the diplomat is blackmailed into helping the spies. The moral conclusion of the film, if there is one in fact,

---

*This is found in a lot of soft porn, *e.g.* Metzger's *The Lickerish Quartet,* where the wife watches herself being turned on by the other woman in a home movie.

9

is that there are no depths to which spying will not sink — the lesbian as sexual object is fair game for whatever exploitation.

The definition of the male homosexual as a sexual object, socially defined as female (the myth, among others, that gay men are passive) threatens the assumption of male active virility. There is no power to be gained from finding out about the mechanics of male homosexuality. The crime of gay men is betrayal of the myth of the 'real man'. Nevertheless, the male homosexual may retain the confidence of the power men have, *i.e.* economically, socially and culturally, but may additionally derive confidence from relating sexually to *other* men with this power. Unlike the lesbian he is not betraying the respect due to male privilege which he also possesses. In this he is far more a victim of heterosexism than sexism, which he is hurt by rather than oppressed by depending on the degree of his identification with a feminine role. Even in the negative attitude towards women, often present in gay men's behaviour, there is basic agreement with patriarchal society. In this context it is not surprising to note in the case of Greece the extent to which male homosexuality was compatible with a patriarchal society.

The artistic sphere has long been claimed by gay men as legitimate territory: in this area the male homosexual has found the means to pass by identifying himself as artistic/romantic rather than simply as gay. So, the social rejection on the basis of sexuality is refocused by the justification of art. Alternatively, sexual illegality leads to a heightened sensibility about the world (and, as argued by Genet, a political one). This contradiction is the one in which all gay art situates itself, and is explored in greater depth in Jack Babuscio's essay.

Avant-garde cinema reflects the Gay Liberation demand for the right to be explicitly homosexual in stating: 'This is what we are, how we see things, what we do; we are a part of life.' The film makers vary widely in their approach: in Kenneth Anger's films homosexuality is situated in a world which is violent and the overtones are sado-masochistic; Gregory Markopoulos' films are introverted and somewhat precious, edited in jarring and rhythmical time and space distortions; the Warhol-Morrissey films are high camp, showing every form of sexuality available on the screen (including non-sexuality, *e.g.* Joe Dallesandro in *Trash*, 1970); and my favourite, Genet's *Chant d'amour,* is lyrical and highly political in its association of repression of homosexuality and abuse of power (*e.g.* in the famous sequence where the voyeuristic guard, unable to ask a prisoner to go down on him, gets off on putting his gun in the man's mouth). There are many other instances of male homosexuality in the American Underground cinema, but the only woman film maker I have found in this group is Shirley Clarke, and her film is also about a gay man (*Portrait of Jason*).

It appears that only the Warhol-Morrissey films pay any attention to lesbians: there are some in *Chelsea Girls* and, later, there is the well-known sequence in *Flesh*, in which Joe Dallesandro, returning from hustling to get money for his wife's girlfriend's abortion, finds them in bed together and is told to 'fuck off'; so, disinterested, he turns over and goes to sleep while they continue to make love next to him. This non-voyeurism, unique in the treatment of lesbians in the cinema, relates to the fact that, on the whole, the consciousness of these films is definitely gay male — even the 'heterosexual couple' in *Trash* are both men, as are most of the *Women in Revolt* (1972). Lesbianism is simply part of 'life's rich tapestry' which seems to consist more of transvestites.

The easy-going treatment of lesbianism in the Warhol-Morrissey films, though not particularly political, contrasts sharply with an English experimental film featuring a lesbian sequence in the (fantasy?) life of its namesake *Suzy Chalk*. This sequence is a voyeuristic rip-off, the better to make the film consumable, and the experimental editing is pure 'arty' gloss. The fact that Ms Chalk apparently suggested this scene, as well as one in which she has a fight with another woman in the street, makes clear the extent to which women may adopt male fantasies (purely sexual or violent relationships with other women) and the extent to which the film maker is either unaware of or disinterested in the mechanics of male oppression.

I feel *Suzy Chalk* demonstrates a trap into which *avant-garde* film could easily fall, in taking its definitions and representations of lesbians from stereotypes and myths, because the primary concern is with form alone rather than also being with content. This political naïvety about content is reflected in the iconographic use of nude women in many recent English *avant-garde* films — a use which one might have expected to be no longer possible in any kind of 'innocent' way, if the film makers were aware of the kind of work done, for example, by John Berger on the objectification of women.[9] Without any political consciousness about the content of film, it is easy for the *avant-garde* to represent lesbianism in a way that has more to do with porn than anything else.

Stereotypes and myths: men's films about lesbians
The myths on which the cinema is based relate to the complex and often contradictory mythology of women, which operates in society as a whole.
Claire Johnston, *Notes on Women's Cinema*

The struggle to change the social and economic conditions of women has all along the line been a struggle with women's own consciousness of their condition, basic to which is a constantly reconditioned sense of powerlessness (either as an individual or collectively). Studies have been made on a wide variety of topics: literature, fashion, psychology, job-conditions, advertising, language, history, etc. that repeatedly show how sexism operates to keep women oppressed. The cinema is included in this brief as it has reflected, and continues to reflect, the expectations and role models available to women.[10]

The contradictory stereotypes that women are expected to fulfil (little girl, sex object, mother, career-girl, goddess, etc. *ad nauseam*) are probably at the root of the possibility for a new women's consciousness: the tensions between these expectations can no longer be glossed over in a rapidly changing

11

society, in which class or social status varies from one generation to the next.[11] None of these options describes a whole person, and the fulfilment of any one of these by one woman has been a task demanding considerable strength and resourcefulness, not to mention a great deal of self-mutilation.

Like other women, lesbians are victims to the twin processes of stereotyping and mythologising. Myths, such as those exploited and perpetrated by porn films ('Lesbians are fantastic in bed' and 'all a lesbian needs is a good screw') although quite contradictory (why should a woman need a screw if her sex life is that good independent of men?) can either be subscribed to independently of each other (as the first is in both *The Kremlin Letter* and *The Lickerish Quartet*) or they can be found together without obvious disjunction *because of their mythical status*. Myths about lesbians have the added value of reflecting on other women: the first of these myths finds straight (heterosexual) women wanting, the second puts all women, gay or straight, onto the same level as sex-objects for men.

The other side of the coin of men's fantasies about lesbians (and women) is quite a deep fund of fear, which finds its expression in representing lesbians as castrating bitches or sadists. These fears serve to maintain divisions between women on the basis of sexual orientation. Looking at the media not one but three lesbian stereotypes emerge:

the butch/mannish lesbian (bar dyke/foot-stomper, often working-class and dominant in her relationships with other women)
the sophisticated lesbian (often an older woman, who is rich and successful in a man's world)
the neurotic lesbian (often *femme* or closet)

Often these stereotypes and fears are combined to form one lesbian character. In *Rome, Open City* the lesbian is at the same time a sophisticated older woman, who is mannish in appearance, and a sadistic castrating bitch (literally, in the scene where the priest is tortured). Like Rosa Klebb, the sadistic dyke in *From Russia with Love* (whose castrating behaviour takes the form of aiming her knife-pointed shoe at Bond's crotch at the end of the film!), the character is at the service of an ideological statement, with the rejection of 'normal' sexuality allied with unacceptable political doctrine: in *Rome, Open City* the lesbian is a Nazi; in *From Russia with Love* she is a Communist.

The Killing of Sister George (as a stage-play written by a man, and as a film directed by a man—as are all of the films in this section) is one of the best-known and apparently respected films about lesbians in England. The reason is not simply the apparent social realism of its approach: the film displays all three of the major stereotypes of lesbians as separate characters, the better to show the repulsiveness of each. Sister George (Beryl Reid) is the essence of revolting butch in her outrageous (often sadistic) dominating behaviour (paralleled by the cloying sentimentality of her television role as a district nurse), while Childie (Susanna York) is the ultimate of the neurotic (regressed) lesbian with her dolls and shyness. In fact both women display psychological imbalance, since George is also a heavy drinker, and is equally capable of childlike behaviour (*e.g.* in her apology to the convent for interfering with some nuns in a taxi). Coral Brown's role, as Mrs. Mercy Croft, is that of the successful and sophisticated career woman, who will take Childie away. Her behaviour also shows her to be the castrating bitch of the film. This trait is particularly apparent in her destruction of George, despite the fact that she is another woman—or is this a contradiction based on George's ambiguous sex role?

There is certainly little or no solidarity between any of the women, consistent with male assumptions about women not getting on together (rooted in their fears about women allying). Lesbianism here is not woman-identification in any way. The voyeuristically necessary seduction scene is as nasty as the women: though it is hard to work out what is happening, the dark setting and strange musical score indicate that it is certainly perverted. The events and the portraits of the three women, drawn as quite emotionally repellent, make no attraction to the idea of lesbianism possible. Little threat is implicit in these women's presence in the world since they are destructive of themselves and each other. This is true even of Mrs. Croft, despite her real power in her job and her ability to pass as a straight (heterosexual) woman, since there is an implication in the final dialogue, when George exposes Childie's age and past, that she too will be destroyed by her lesbianism in relating to Childie, even if she discards her newly acquired lover rapidly.

Les biches, The Fox, The Bitter Tears of Petra von Kant, also fit into the freak show *genre,* as do other 'lesbian films' (including, narratively and visually, Bergman's *The Silence* and *Persona*).

Les biches, given the possible misreading of this title in English as 'The Bitches', could have been renamed for US and UK distribution—though of course a straight translation to 'The Does' would not have been clear, but renaming is common practice with foreign films and it is interesting to note that in this case the original title was kept. It is in keeping with the unpleasantness of the lesbian relationship in the film, to which the actual meaning of the French title created a sharp contrast.

Les biches picks up where *Sister George* leaves off with the rich sophisticated predatory older woman picking up an innocent young girl from the streets; the theme is stereotypically overdetermined from the start. With superb film artistry the director shows the playing out of the destruction of innocence, pulling heavily both on voyeuristic interest in lesbian love-making, and the myth that 'all a lesbian needs is a good screw'. Ultimately Frédérique abandons Why for a young man, and Why, maddened by her rejection by both lovers (Paul was originally interested in her) knifes (note the Freudian overtones) her 'protector' and assumes the woman's identity.

Two of these themes recur in *The Bitter Tears of Petra von Kant*: tears cried over Karen, the 'innocent', who turns out to be in it for what she can get and becomes more and more disinterested in her lover, taunting her with her affairs with men, as the older woman becomes less dominating and more and more impassioned with her. Throughout the film Petra, the fashion-designer, assumes and discards wigs, make-up, and clothes, and in this case it is she, the older woman, who eventually dresses up to look like Karen, assuming the identity of the woman who has left her. The unwholesomeness of both women, and the treatment of their environment (totally hermetic, the action never leaving the flat) can be sharply contrasted with Fassbinder's treatment of male homosexual society and its exploited hero in *Fox and his Friends*: Fox, a working-class gay like Karen, is exploited and betrayed by his bourgeois lover rather than the other way round. Furthermore the film emphasises the involvement in the world of gay men with the action taking place in a multitude of milieux, and events like the reappearance of the florist in a gay bar. From this comparison it appears that male gay film makers are no more sympathetic to lesbians than straight ones.

The use of stereotyping in Rydell's *The Fox*, tied in with the myth of a lesbian's need for a man, is at first apparently more complex: the women are more or less the same age and the 'true' lesbian is portrayed in the neurotic *'femme' genre*. March, who will become prey for the 'fox', is the mannish one, though dominated through emotional blackmail by the other woman. The switch is an interesting one in the psychology of the writer (Lawrence),[12] which in the film dominates that of the director. March's assimilation of the male role, particularly in her work around the farm, points to an energy and strength in harmony with nature, which suggests that she is more in touch with her true self than Banford, and more ready to be seduced by Henry.

The disgust felt for the lesbian 'not being a real woman' is often conjoined with a certain fascination. There is of course the 'saviour instinct' that comes into play (a lesbian is just a woman like any other) but there is also the fact that certain lesbians, by absorbing 'male traits' of energy, activity in the world, even a certain 'virility', are seen by some men as more desirable, *because of an apparent masculinity,* reflecting a strong element of repressed homosexuality in these men. By conquering such a woman, not only is the man's uncertainty about his masculinity reassured, but he is even more of a 'real man' because of the difficulty of his successful endeavour. He may choose to ignore that what attracted him was the masculinity of the woman. This is evidenced pretty clearly in the writings of Ian Fleming and their film versions—remember the magical conversion of Pussy Galore in *Goldfinger?*

As pointed out in the previous section, the lesbian is doubly defined by her sexuality, but inasmuch as she is made available to men (or to one man) she is simply 'cunt' (Pussy Galore?!?). The violence to which Emmanuelle must eventually be subjected is also the fate of other non-lesbian but apparently liberated women in modern cinema when they appear at all (*e.g.* in *Klute* [1971], *Frenzy* [1972], and many 'police' films) when they do not succeed in coming to a bad end by their own devices (*e.g.* Mrs. Miller's opium addiction at the end of *McCabe and Mrs. Miller* [1971]). The message in all these films remains that the free choice of sexuality by women choosing not to marry is something that society will punish. Even good wives do not always escape being made sexually available to violent men, as in *Straw Dogs* (1972) or *Clockwork Orange* (1971), and rape appears to be the responsibility of the woman for marrying a weak man. In this it seems that the female stereotypes of good woman and bad woman (wife, whore and lesbian) are merging in a way that makes a general hatred of women's sexuality more blatant than it ever was when protected by a general subscription to domesticity.

Apparently more sympathetic views of lesbians in the cinema are present in the works of three other male film makers: *The Loudest Whisper, The Conformist*, and *Thérèse and Isabelle*. The lesbians in *The Loudest Whisper* and *The Conformist* are both portrayed with a certain stereotyping: Shirley MacLaine's character, Martha, is a neurotic (closet) lesbian; Dominique Sanda as Anna Quadri is sophisticated and bourgeois. Thésèse and Isabelle are both safely unstereotyped, being schoolgirls.

Despite her stereotyping, Martha in *The Loudest Whisper* is sympathetically portrayed because the concept that she is dangerous and predatory (a child molester) is attacked by the film's exposure of society's paranoia. The film is important in that there is solidarity between the two woman, and a certain ambivalence is found in Karen's behaviour since she is not anxious to leave her life with Martha in order to get married — she even brings her along on dates with her fiancé. (In the end she decides not to marry him, so the film does not use lesbianism to service heterosexuality.) It is the self-disgust of the realisation that she really is a lesbian that causes Martha to commit suicide. In doing this she remains a victim of her society to the end, having internalised its rejection of homosexuality. It is useful to note that this film is based on a play by a woman, Lillian Hellman, which goes a long way in explaining its positive aspects. As a film, however, it was made just after the McCarthy era and one feels it is as much a statement against the régime of false rumour spreading and intolerance of deviance as it is about lesbianism, which never appears as a valid option.

The interests of *The Conformist* are definitely elsewhere: in the psychological and social pressures that make Marcello Clerici (Trintignant) a fascist capable of being responsible for the deaths of people he admires and loves. Anna Quadri's sympathetic portrayal is in part due to her attractiveness, and in part due to the fact that she is anti-fascist and victim. However, her initial overstated 'butchness' (at the Quadri's house and also in her dancing lesson) and her predatory behaviour towards the stereotypically silly Giulia (who plays the feminine role to the hilt) show her in a less positive light: as a bored bourgeoise, she is a long way from the street vendor who sings the Internationale or the ordinary working people at the dance. The key to the film is in Bertolucci's attitude to the bourgeoisie and its impotence. There is even a certain ambiguity in Anna's relationship with Clerici, which seems made up of a stated revulsion and an unstated fascination (the myth that 'every woman loves a fascist' covering 'all a lesbian needs . . .'?) The film is better at shedding light on the male characters than on the female ones, and their attitude to Anna's lesbianism is instructive: Professor Quadri's attitude is purely voyeuristic ('They are so beautiful'); Clerici's is the desire to conquer, wishing to see Anna as a sex-object, like his wife, and her role in the film is partly to emphasise his repressed homosexuality, already hinted at in his guilt about the childhood incident with the chauffeur. Her final shooting indicates the sorry end to which decadent bourgeois lesbians must come.

Thérèse and Isabelle is quite a different kettle of fish, apparently, being based on Violet Leduc's autobiographical novel of the same name (a fragment of which appears in *La bâtarde* [1938]) and is exclusively about the relationship between two girls at boarding school (those notorious hotbeds of adolescent lesbianism!!), a relationship where no patterns of dominance emerge, and where both emotions and sexuality are on a give-and-take basis. Unfortunately three factors betray the film as unliberated in its attitude to the girls: the fact that they are played by two actresses clearly out of their teens; the graphic and beautiful portrayal of their sexual encounters (which clearly puts the film in the soft porn *genre*); and the fact that the events are in the memory of one of the women about to marry and settle into her correct role in life. It was 'just a phase they were going through' like Emmanuelle, March, and countless others in hard porn flicks.

In general it appears that despite the emergence of a new consciousness about gayness and womanity, the cinema is entrenched in viewing both as negative and potentially destructive (either of self or others) unless a safe domesticity prevails in marriage to a 'strong' man.

Lesbians at the movies

I myself never go to the cinema or hardly ever practically and the cinema has never read my work or hardly ever. Gertrude Stein,[13] *Plays*

As an ever greater number of lesbians come out (live out their gayness openly), film makers are cashing in on this market as well by producing explicitly lesbian films for mass audiences. But how do we lesbians respond, react, feel and think about these films and others?

I remember being depressed for days after seeing *Sister George*, feeling: 'Sure, such a relationship may exist, but what a miserable one, and what's it doing on film to pervert young minds about lesbians? Why not a film of the *Ladies of Llangollen?'** I talked with a friend, who said she thought it was a good film, well acted and all, but she was furious at the stereotyping. Others enjoyed some of George's outrageous anti-establishment behaviour (particularly the incident with the nuns) and others yet spoke of the character played by Coral Brown as a turn-on (the myth of the sophisticated older woman rules OK apparently); but the general impression was a certain unease, despite the desire to have a film that was lesbian.

The only other widely seen film of this group (apart from *The Fox*, which in no way is claimed as a lesbian film), *Emmanuelle*, seems to have had a similar response. Despite the pleasure felt at the ease of the relationship between Emmanuelle and Bee and the rarity of seeing lesbian sex so positively

*By Elisabeth Mabor, Penguin, 1973.

depicted, there is a general feeling that the film is a rip-off, basically geared to a straight audience both in its *Vogue* glossy sophisticated innocence and its 'moral' ending. This becomes particularly apparent in trying to explain the way in which Bee leaves Emmanuelle to her fate with little or no concern over her future. This heterosexual model of playboy behaviour ('The adventure is over, bye-bye.') simply does not ring true in women's relationships to each other; the small details that we are given to characterise Bee (a sensitive woman, who has achieved a certain independence of men in her work) are not consistent with such a lack of concern. One simply feels the need of the director to wind up the affair in order to get back to the nitty-gritty.

On the whole, lesbians' interest in the cinema seems to be oriented towards those exceptional films made in Hollywood during the late 1930s and 40s, when the needs of the patriarchy/capitalism to make war and money demanded that women be orientated away from home-making and into industry to replace men sent away as cannon-fodder. These films often had as central characters strong and resilient women, played by such actresses as Lauren Bacall, Joan Crawford, Bette Davis, Marlene Dietrich, Greta Garbo, Katharine Hepburn and Barbara Stanwyck. More recently, the cowgirl films (*Annie Get Your Gun* [1950], *Calamity Jane* [1953], etc.) and films with Jeanne Moreau and Glenda Jackson enjoy some such popularity.

The popularity of these films is consistent with my having defined lesbianism primarily as woman-identification. There is a real need for lesbians to see and know about women who define themselves in their own terms. In the strength of actresses often playing parts in which they are comparatively independent of domestic expectations and of men is found a far greater affirmation than in the kind of 'lesbian films' that have been produced. Most lesbians have been through a heterosexual phase, so the plot demand that the heroine be attracted to a man is not particularly disturbing (irritating maybe), and the explanation for the plot development could lie in the fact that there is no woman around of equal strength to attract the heroine . . .

In the few Hollywood films of the 1930s and 40s where any kind of overt lesbianism is apparent it is treated in an episodic, almost irrelevant fashion (except that it has the function of making the heroine even more attractive to the men in the film, giving rise to both repressed homosexuality and the conqueror instinct discussed previously). Marlene Dietrich is famous for her appearance in drag in her film-stage numbers, but significantly less remembered for her flirtations with the women in her audiences in *Blonde Venus* (1932) and *Morocco* (1930). Both Katharine Hepburn and Garbo have also appeared on film in men's clothing. In *Sylvia Scarlett* (1935) Katharine Hepburn, dressed as a boy, is approached by a young woman who playfully draws a moustache on Sylvia's lip and kisses her; Sylvia jumps up and runs away. In *Queen Christina* (1933), a rewrite of the life of the famous Swedish lesbian queen who gave up her throne rather than marry, Garbo is initially involved in an affair with her chambermaid and the two even kiss quite passionately on the screen; the lovers argue and separate, leaving the bulk of the film to be taken up with a heterosexual affair (but how lesbians cheer when

17

Garbo says 'I want to be alone'!).
Janet Meyers, discussing this phenomenon, says of these three stars:

> Most lesbians I know feel a strong response to these women on screen. The qualities they projected, of being inscrutable to the men in the films and aloof, passionate, direct, could not be missed. They are all strong, tough and yet genuinely tender. In short, though rarely permitted to hint it, they are lesbians. Because of the old star system in the Hollywood studios, where movie projects were 'created' to suit particular stars, that lesbian reality surfaced in memorable ways.[14]

Positive and self-reliant women in modern Hollywood cinema are more rare — and, as pointed out earlier, usually punished for unsocial behaviour. *Alice* (who) *Doesn't Live Here Any More* (1974), in a film made as a sop to the new feminist consciousness, is a poor substitute for Amanda in *Adam's Rib* (1949), a woman who chooses to even risk her marriage to a man she genuinely loves (appositely played by Spencer Tracy) over a question of true feminist principle: she decides to defend a deserted wife against the charge of trying to murder her husband. The support of other women in Alice's search for a self-determined identity is either non-existent or insufficient. The fact that she gives up her struggle in the arms of 'a good man' makes the film obvious for what it is: a reiteration of the values of patriarchal society. It is not surprising that lesbians find little of positive value in contemporary films in general distribution.

Although European art film is no less bound by patriarchal culture, the lack of an overt consensus about 'what will sell' or what the content should be has given European directors a greater freedom of fantasy about the identity of women and about their search for a self-identity. The fact remains that the 'identity', their 'search' and 'self-identity' are seen in relation to men and the male-defined world, though the mode of representation of women has often been realist. This has resulted in female roles that are far more overtly mysterious or childlike. The qualities implied in these stereotypes make it possible for feminists to analyse a wide range of unconscious male fears, desires and intentions. This area remains relatively unexplored by feminists given that feminist film culture emerged at a time when Hollywood was the cinema being assessed.

Céline et Julie vont en bateau (1974) stands in sharp contrast to these films, in its de-emphasis on men. The few men in the film are sent up: exchanging identities, Céline goes off to unmask Guilou, Julie's ex-boyfriend, as an empty sentimental fringe intellectual and to thwart his marriage plans for Julie; meanwhile Julie stands in for Céline at an audition for a middle-eastern tour, and ends up insulting the men as voyeurs and worse. The film is delightful in describing an easy-going trouble-free relationship between women. There is no overt homosexuality in the film, but it can be seen as an (unconscious) organising factor. There is nothing explicitly sexual in their relationship, but they play together a lot and are very physical. They have apparently not only gone away (as the title indicates) from their normal lives, but also from social expectations that demand that they identify themselves in relation to men.

Céline and Julie are well on the way to becoming woman-identified women in play that has a political bite to it.* By not being overtly homosexual, their relationship is saved from voyeuristic interest and other facets of women relating to each other positively are explored in greater depth.

The question of homosexuality in film is not simply that of its expression, but also that of its repression. This operates in the most surprising films and the examination of films in terms of their sexual implications (for example psychoanalytic readings) could do well to note this factor.

Women (lesbians?) make films about women (lesbians?): rejections of hetero-sexuality, the option of lesbianism

There is genius in the veins of women and it flows full tide, but under-ground.   Nelly Kaplan
Are these women lesbians?
        Red Moon Rising, film in production with Penny Holland.

In the past the limitations of films by men about women have, on the whole, also been found in women's films. Feminist analysis of the cinema, however, has begun to show ways in which feminist attitudes come through, even in apparently male-identified films (such as those of Dorothy Arzner[15]), as well as discovering a *her*story of film which has been largely ignored or dismissed by male critics.[16]

On research and analysis quite a number of women's films show evidence of criticism and dissatisfaction with women's assumed roles at the service of patriarchy. Rejection of the assumptions of the heterosexual norm as destructive and shallow, implicit in *Céline et Julie . . .*, is present in many women's films from the *avant-garde* (Germaine Dulac[17] and Maya Deren) to Hollywood (Dorothy Arzner), through European art film (Mai Zetterling's *The Girls* [1972], Mireille Dansereau's *La vie rêvée,* Anja Breien's *Wives* [1975], etc.).

In Germaine Dulac's *La coquille et le clergyman* (1929), filmed totally in experimental style until the final sequence, we find a series of male fantasies about the mystery of Woman, her attractiveness and repulsiveness, the conquest of a rival, being subverted by the grotesqueness of the 'hero'. The cut back to reality in which he is gasping and choking on air puts the final lid on the impotent ridiculousness of his fantasy life. The film was universally repudiated by the surrealists ('It is a FEMININE film' wrote Ado Kyrou[18]), led by Artaud, who wrote the original script, for 'de-virilising' his intent. Subsequent critical dislike of the film appears to stem from the same source.

*The script was a genuine collaboration written with the two main actresses, Juliet Berto and Dominique Labourier, as well as Bulle Ogier and Marie-France Pisier, who also appear in the film.

No male critic has recognised the importance of what Germaine Dulac was doing.[19]

The same theme of men's obsession with their fantasised image of Woman came up again a couple of years later in a little known film made in England by Elinor Glyn called *Knowing Men*. It was described at the time by the London *Daily Mail* as 'depicting man as possessing one characteristic only which compels him to ogle, then maul every woman he meets'.[20] The use of mockery, found in many of these films, is an ongoing tradition, also present in Mai Zetterling's *The Girls,* and Vera Chytilova's *Daisies* (1966) amongst others.

An approach that shows heterosexuality as far more threatening and ultimately destructive is found in Maya Deren's *Meshes of the Afternoon* (1943). This film can be read purely as poetic imagery of sexuality. Initially the young woman is sitting masturbating looking out of the window, but instead of following her physical exploration of herself, we are led to follow a dark cloaked figure into the gardens that surround the house (this figure who often holds objects, such as a rose, a key, scissors, and whose face is a mirror, seems to be the unconscious sexuality of the woman herself). Time and space dilate and retract, objects and figures appear and disappear. When the woman returns to the house she finds a man and the tension (of the more threatening objects, the difficulties of opening the door) becomes violence. The scissors reappear, a knife, a mirror is broken, the woman killed. The last shot of the sequence could be from a film about a rape victim; the woman lies dead, strangled by her telephone cord. The lyricism of the autoeroticism has been completely destroyed by the intrusion of the man.

The option of seeing heterosexual assumptions and practices as destructive is not the only one however — they can also be viewed as void of interest. This is the direction taken in Mireille Dansereau's *La vie rêvée*: the dream life of the title is the fantasy that two women weave around one of the women's attraction towards a man she has not even met; she finally does meet him and takes him to bed with her, only to be totally disappointed. In the final scene the two women joyfully tear their collage of male and romantic pin-ups off the walls.

None of these films, despite the scorn, disinterest and genuine fear with which men's behaviour and expectations are shown, ever resolve themselves by offering lesbianism as a positive alternative for the definition of one's womanself — though this is indicated, if one is able to see it, in the endings of both *La vie rêvée* and *Wives*; the women have sincerely begun to redefine themselves in positive terms and will not be returning to their old male-identified ideas and lives (as Mai Zetterling's *Girls* appear to be doing at the end of her film).

Among the few films about lesbianism made by women before the emergence of the Women's Movement are Leontine Sagan's *Mädchen in Uniform* and Jacqueline Audry's *Olivia, Huis clos* and *La garçonne*. The original sources of the first two were also written by women: *Mädchen in Uniform* was a play by Christa Winsloe, and *Olivia* is based on an autobiographical novel of the same name with a screenplay by Colette. Both films are set in boarding schools and the theme is the young heroine's passion for a warm and caring teacher; both films are about love rather than sex — and thus unvoyeuristic. Here the similarity ends. The schools are completely different: Manuela's is a training ground to instil *Kinder, Küche, Kirche** in girls who, like her, are not conforming; whilst Olivia's French finishing school bathes in an atmosphere of charm and ease, and education is approached as a pleasure.

Mädchen in Uniform is a powerful indictment of Nazi mentality and its attempts to crush individuality — and some criticisms I have read of it limit themselves entirely to this facet, burying the lesbianism of its content. Yet it is precisely in the way that the film links Manuela's anti-authoritarianism and her lesbianism, and the way in which the other girls ally themselves with her, that the statement is most powerful. This is also the only feature-length lesbian film not to have an obligatory sad ending: in the home-market version Manuela succeeds in killing herself; in the version made for non-Nazi audiences the teacher and girls succeed in saving her.

Leontine Sagan's film is also remarkable in the fact that it was one of the first films to be made collectively (socialism and feminism in Germany had been apparently the strongest in Europe at that time). The fate of the director is shrouded in mystery: it is known that she fled to England, where she made one more film, *Men of Tomorrow,* for Alex Korda in 1932, but nothing further.

Jacqueline Audry, on the other hand, has a rich filmography (16 films between 1943 and 1970, many of them adaptations of famous works including *Gigi* [1949], and *Huis clos*).

Olivia is not a political film in the way *Mädchen* is. It can be read as defining the limits to which the ruling class will allow its women to go to become charming wives or mistresses. The film, of course, had a sad ending with the beloved Mlle. Julie dying broken by the jealousy of the co-owner of the school, Mlle. Cara. Despite all this the film remains a celebration of a gentle world of women-loving-women, but as such it has been safely buried in the history of the cinema.

Equally well-buried is a more recent film scripted, financed and originally written by Christiane Rochefort (see also *Warrior's Rest*) called *Les stances à Sophie*. Not only are the two young wives, Céline and Julia, totally bored with and mocking of their bourgeois husbands, involving themselves in a number of subversive projects — like many of the women in films belonging to this section — but they also become lovers. Christiane Rochefort herself is not so interested in lesbianism ('The women are playing'[21] — like Céline and Julie in the Rivette film which the book predates by some years?) as much as male-identification, and the way that patriarchy co-opts love: when Julia dies, killed by her husband in a car accident, Céline accuses him of murder; yet, despite her own husband's complicity, she still believes she loves him and does not leave until some time later as he continues to glory in his possession and control of her in a series of psychological sadistic acts.

The question remains—despite social disapproval of lesbianism—why there were so few lesbian films by gay women in the past. We know, from Parker

*Children, Kitchen, Church.

Tyler's *Screening the Sexes* and Kenneth Anger's *Hollywood Babylon*,[22] that a large number of lesbians were involved in the film making process in Hollywood, and this is probably no less true elsewhere. The explanation partly lies in the lack of support from an alliance of lesbians proud and open enough about their lifestyle to be reckoned with as a social force (gayness was for a long time either a completely private matter or outlawed in small communities), but it mainly rests in the absence of strong political rather than personal reasons to make lesbian films. Trying to make feminist statements in film was hard enough, as the incomprehension and anger that Germaine Dulac's films faced illustrate, but to do so in terms of lesbianism was asking for total rejection. *Mädchen in Uniform* is an important exception to this generalisation.

The recent emergence of lesbianfeminism has changed this situation radically: there are clearly now pressing political reasons for woman-identified women to make films in relation to their politics, and a growing audience for explicitly political lesbian films. A few women have made a start in this direction.

In *Film as a Subversive Art*,[23] Amos Vogel's chapter on homosexuality and other taboos in the cinema only finds one lesbian making explicitly lesbian films: Constance Beeson, whose films are, according to him, quite lyrical (*Holding*). Her films also explore sexuality in both bisexual (*The Now* [1970]) and heterosexual terms (*Unfolding*, which Vogel wrongly implies is lesbian in content) and she has recently made a number of overtly feminist films (*The Doll, High on Drag* and *Women*). In the lyrical vein there is also Virginia Giritlian's *Cumulus Nimbus*, a short about a woman deciding to begin a lesbian love affair.[24] Barbara Hammer's image-associative lesbian films (*Sisters, A Gay Day, X* and *Dyketactics*) are more widely known, having been shown around the US at different women's events and spaces.

On the whole, the tendency of Women's Movement films has been towards documentary style 'letting the real women speak for themselves' (though this raises political problems in the assumption of film as 'pure' objective recording device) — reflecting its own development through consciousness-raising and respect for personal experience as political. Lesbian films in this *genre* include one of Kate Millet and Louva Irvine's *Three Lives* (co-makers Susan Kleckner and Robin Mide), the Berkeley Lesbian Feminist Film Collective's *Coming Out*, Elaine Jacob's *Lavender*, Sherrie Farrell's *Sandy and Madeline's Family*, as well as a film in the making by Iris Films about lesbian mothers.

More interesting is the work of Jan Oxenberg, whose two lesbian films *Home Movie* and *A Comedy in Six Unnatural Acts* have had quite a lot of acclaim in the US Women's Movement. She uses humour to look at stereotypes and expectations of lesbianism and is currently involved in making a film about a daughter and mother. Her work combines positive attitudes to lesbianism with a critical look at film itself, as recording device (*Home Movie*), and as mood manipulator (*Comedy . . .*).

In *Home Movie* the filmmaker in voice-over talks about the filmed images of herself as a child ('Can anyone tell this child will grow up as a lesbian?'), a teenage cheer leader and an adult demonstrating and playing with other lesbians: her story, before coming out, is apparently that of a typical middle-American girl growing up (why isn't there a myth that the girl next door could be a lesbian? She often was, and increasingly is.)

A Comedy in Six Unnatural Acts attacks stereotypes directly, representing each 'act' (foot-stomping dyke in action, child molester, etc.) in the style of a particular cinematic convention (1950s 'B' pictures, romance, heroic adventure and so on). The myths perpetrated so 'subtly' by the media are thus exposed for what they are, no more real than the forms in which they are presented, and by provoking laughter at the relentless series the film maker gives us the right to examine their implications whilst dismissing their power to control women's lives.

Concluding notes

In describing lesbianism as woman-identification, I have given myself a wider brief in my discussion than simply to analyse films from the point of view of women sexually orientated towards women. The power structure that restricts all women's roles in the cinema is one that delimits the roles of lesbians, making it hard to see lesbianism in any other terms than sexual. Conversely, because of the political nature of an anti-social choice of sexuality by women the way films do represent lesbians is highly relevant to all women: the kinds of myths, stereotypes and plots of 'lesbian films' reflect the need of patriarchal capitalist society to divide in order to rule. A way to do this is to make both heterosexism (in the representation of homosexuality) and sexism (in the representation of women) appear natural. Film is an excellent vehicle for this strategy in its pretension to reality, dependent on our conditioned acceptance of the meaning of film language, hiding behind the notion of simple entertainment. 'Lesbian films' are clearly made for the general public and serve to reinforce negative images of lesbianism—as such, few lesbians find anything to identify with in these films, whose purpose is to continue to support the *status quo*. These films fulfil voyeuristic desires whilst warning women to stay in safe heterosexual domesticty, despite the implied inadequacy of their own sexual competence.

As I have pointed out, on the whole, lesbians (and indeed feminists) are attracted by films containing independent and sensitive strong women, but a frustration for lesbians in watching such films is the potential lesbianism of the heroine(s) which never surfaces. It would be pleasant to see a film in general distribution using a traditional Hollywood plot of the type in which a self-sufficient heroine *does something* (saves the firm from bankruptcy, organises a successful strike, or whatever) with a male peer who, come the inevitable romantic ending, suggests they 'get hitched'; she replies, 'Sorry, I'm not interested. I have no intention of involving myself in such oppressive relationships. I'm a lesbian', and walks off into the sunset either alone or with another woman! This little fantasy on a well-worn plot (variations are endless, as Hollywood discovered) serves to emphasise a point made by Joan Mellen[25] that lesbians are rarely represented in films as having anything more important to do than deal with their relationships—their work, when they have any (such as Petra von Kant's designing or Mrs. Croft's job in television administration), is of minimal interest except inasmuch as it highlights their perversity (*e.g.* George's sugary television role). Indeed, unless a woman's lesbianism is a closely-guarded secret it becomes a major known fact about her life: Vita Sackville-West is better known nowadays as a lesbian than as either a gardener or a novelist. The taboo nature of homosexuality made it for a long time an unknown fact (how many people realised that Gertrude Stein was a lesbian?), but now there is scurrilous interest (was Virginia Woolfe really a lesbian?); although this is perhaps an improvement on invisibility it remains negative and is paralleled by the type of greater visibility of lesbians in modern cinema.

The representation of lesbianism in a fairly positive light is beginning to show signs of happening, even within mainstream cinema as in Jacqueline Susann's *Once is not Enough,* where the lesbian relationship is the most positive and warm one in the film. However, in none of the recent films is lesbianism explored in terms of being a rejection of the female role or social expectations of 'femininity': in *Once is not Enough* the women are married and display all the attributes of femininity in dress, make-up etc. While a number of women's films have shown up the destructiveness or ridiculousness of men's behaviour and expectations, only the recent *Les stances à Sophie* goes in the direction of positing relationships between women as a creative alternative in searching for an independent identity. Céline emerges from her experience of love and marriage somewhat scarred, but with another life to lead somewhere else, a true 'culture heroine', transcending both the feminine qualities that her marriage required of her and the 'male' qualities of strength and endurance, to a will to struggle and win in her own terms. Like *La fiancée du pirate*, still unavailable in 16mm, the limited distribution of the film, despite its conventional form, points to an assumed lack of general interest in its subject matter, and an inability to know how to market the film because of the unacceptability of its politics. Christiane Rochefort has said regarding distribution:

> It's important to see that it's not just the monetary motive—the fact that they will show anything if they believe they can make money by it—because there is a limit and that limit is sexism.[26]

However, as Claire Johnston so correctly points out,[27] the work of feminist film makers should not limit itself to replacing heroes of the patriarchy with feminist heroines, although this is an important and necessary part of a feminist film struggle. If we are concerned about the way that film promotes its illusions, then there is a need to reflect in our film making practice on these devices and strategies (as Jan Oxenberg has begun to do in *Home Movie* and, with the help of the lesbian community, in *Comedy in Six Unnatural Acts*). This work of analysis and negation of the way patriarchal culture operates in film to buttress the unthinkingness of male fears and fantasies (in women as well as men) is a first step in developing and affirming a new consciousness which may eventually produce a radically different women's film language. Inasmuch as women are beginning to establish the ways in which the language is male in its assumptions they are also discovering that this is true of film language. This essay has been an early discussion of a certain filmic vocabulary related to lesbianism. The search for a woman's language in all domains (science, poetry etc.) is one that is also taking place in film. It is one that will only take place in the public eye if a wider variety of films are in general distribution and the techniques of film criticism and film making are in the hands of that very public.

Notes

1. Engels, F. 'The Origins of the Family, Private Property and the State', Pathfinder Press, New York, 1972.
2. Cf Juliet Mitchell, *Psychoanalysis and Feminism,* Pelican Press, London, 1975, particularly Chs. 6 'Pre-oedipal Sexuality' and 12 'The Marks of Womanhood'.
3. Cf Claire Johnston, 'Towards a Feminist Film Practice: Some Theses' in *Edinburgh' 76 Magazine* (Psycho-analysis/Cinema/Avant-Garde); also Dr. Charlotte Woolf's observation of greater homoemotionality in women, in *Love Between Women,* Duckworth Press, London, 1971.
4. From an article on rape which appeared in *Nova.*
5. Ti-Grace Atkinson 'Lesbianism and Feminism' in Phyllis Birkby, Bertha Harris, Jill Johnston, Ester Newton and Jane O'Wyatt (eds.), *Amazon Expedition*, Times Change Press, New York, 1973; also on this topic, 'The woman identified woman' by Radicalesbians in Phil Brown (ed.), *Radical Psychology*, Tavistock Press, London, 1973; and *Lesbianism and the Women's Movement*, Diana Press, Baltimore, Maryland, 1974.
6. Ti-Grace Atkinson, op. cit.
7. For example, *Class and Feminism*, Diana Press, Baltimore, Maryland, 1974; or the quarterly journal *Quest* (Washington D.C.).
8. See Laura Mulvey, 'Visual Pleasure and Narrative Cinema', *Screen*, Vol. 16, No. 3, Autumn 1975, p6.
9. John Berger, *Ways of Seeing,* BBC and Pelican, London, 1972.
10. *E.g.* the journal *Women and Film* (Berkeley, California, 4 issues, 1973-75, no longer in publication); Claire Johnston (ed.), *Notes on Women's Cinema*, SEFT; Molly Haskell, *From Reverence to Rape*, Penguin, 1974; Joan Mellen, *Women and their Sexuality in the New Film*, Horizon Press, New York, 1973; Marjorie Rosen, *Popcorn Venus*, Avon Books, New York, 1974; Musidora, *Paroles . . . elles tournent*, Librairie des Femmes, Paris, 1976; as well as a number of articles in feminist journals all over the world, including *Spare Rib* (London).
11. 'Wherever there is a general attempt on the part of the women of a society to readjust their position in it, a close analysis will always show the changed or changing conditions of that society have made women's acquiescence no longer necessary or desirable', quoted from Olive Scheiner, Introduction to *Women and Labour,* 1911, in *Dyke*, Spring 1976 (New York).
12. Cf Kate Millet's analysis of D. H. Lawrence in *Sexual Politics*, Paladin.
13. Recently two very interesting feminist films were made by California film makers, Roberta Friedman and Graham Weinbren of the Oasis group: *The Making Of Americans,* based on a section of the book of the same name by Gertrude Stein, and *Bertha's Children.*
14. Janet Meyers, 'Dyke Goes To The Movies', *Dyke,* (New York) Spring 1976, p. 38.
15. Karen Kay and Gerald Peary, 'Dorothy Arzner's *Dance Girl Dance*', in *Velvet Light Trap*, No. 10, Fall 1973; Claire Johnston (ed.), *The Work Of Dorothy Arzner: Towards a Feminist Cinema*, BFI, London, 1974.
16. Try searching for women film makers in the index of film books; or did you know that the first short fiction film may have been made by Alice Guy Blache rather than Méliès?
17. See William van Wert, 'Germaine Dulac: First Feminist Film Maker', *Women and Film,* Nos. 5-6.

18. Ibid p.57.
19. Bar William van Wert, of course, but see, for example: J. H. Matthew, *Surrealism and Film,* University of Michigan Press, 1971, pp.78-80; Raymond Durgnat, *Sexual Alienation in the Cinema*, Studio Vista, London, 1972, p.250. For a critique of the surrealists and sexism see Xavière Gautier, *Le suréalisme et la sexualité*, Paris, 1976.
20. Sharon Smith, 'Women Who Make Movies', in *Women and Film*, Nos. 3-4, p.85.
21. 'An Interview with Christiane Rochefort', in *Women and Film*, Nos. 3-4.
22. Parker Tyler, *Screening the Sexes*, Anchor Doubleday, New York, 1973; Kenneth Anger, *Hollywood Babylon*, Associated Professional Services, Phoenix, 1965.
23. Amos Vogel, 'The Breaking of Sexual Taboos: homosexuality and other variants', in *Film As A Subversive Art*, Weidenfeld and Nicolson, London, 1974.
24. Cf Bonnie Dawson, *Women's Films in Print*, Bootlegger Press, San Francisco, 1975.
25. Joan Mellen, 'Lesbianism in the Movies', in *Women and Their Sexuality in the New Film.*
26. 'An interview with Christiane Rochefort', op. cit.
27. Claire Johnston, 'Introduction', *Notes on Women's Cinema*, op. cit.

Stereotyping

by Richard Dyer

Gay people, whether activists or not, have resented and attacked the images of homosexuality in films (and the other arts and media) for as long as we have managed to achieve any self-respect. (Before that, we simply accepted them as true and inevitable). The principle line of attack has been on stereotyping.

The target is a correct one. There is plenty of evidence [1] to suggest that stereotypes are not just put out in books and films, but are widely agreed upon and believed to be right. Particularly damaging is the fact that many gay people believe them, leading on the one hand to the self-oppression so characteristic of gay people's lives,[2] and on the other to behaviour in conformity with the stereotypes which of course only serves to confirm their truth. Equally, there can be no doubt that most stereotypes of gays in films are demeaning and offensive. Just think of the line-up—the butch dyke and the camp queen, the lesbian vampire and the sadistic queer, the predatory schoolmistress and the neurotic faggot, and all the rest. The amount of hatred, fear, ridicule and disgust packed into those images is unmistakable.

But we cannot leave the question of stereotyping at that. Just as recent work on images of blacks and women has done,[3] thinking about images of gayness needs to go beyond simply dismissing stereotypes as wrong and distorted. Righteous dismissal does not make the stereotypes go away, and tends to prevent us from understanding just what stereotypes are, how they function, ideologically and aesthetically, and why they are so resilient in the face of our rejection of them. In addition, there is a real problem as to just what we would put in their place. It is often assumed that the aim of character construction should be the creation of 'realistic individuals', but, as I will argue, this may have as many drawbacks as its apparent opposite, 'unreal' stereotypes, and some form of typing may actually be preferable to it. These then are the issues that I want to look at in this article—the definition and function of stereotyping and what the alternatives to it are.

Ideology and types

How do we come to our 'understanding' of the people we encounter, in fiction as in life? We get our information about them partly from what other people tell us—although we may not necessarily trust this—and, in fiction, from narrators and from the 'thoughts' of the characters, but most of our knowledge about them is based on the evidence in front of us: what they do and how they do it, what they say and how they say it, dress, mannerisms, where they live and so on. That is where the information comes from—but how do we make sense of it? Sociological theory suggests four different, though inter-related, ways of organising this information: *role, individual, type* and *member*.[4] When we regard a person in their *role*, we are thinking of them purely in terms of the particular set of actions (which I take to include dress, speech and gesture) that they are performing at the moment we encounter them. Thus I may walk down the street and see a road-sweeper, a housewife, a child, an OAP, a milkman. I know from what they are doing what their social role is, and I know, because I live in this society, that that role is defined by what sociologists call 'variables' of occupation, gender, age and kinship. Although this notion of role has developed within a tradition of sociology that views social structure as neutral (not founded upon power and inequality), it is nonetheless valuable because it allows us to distinguish, theoretically at least, between what people do and what they are. However we seldom in practice stop at that, and role usually forms the basis for other inferences we make about people we encounter. We can see a person in the totality of her/his roles—their sum total, specific combination and interaction—a totality that we call an *individual*, complex, specific, unique. Or we can see a person according to a logic that assumes a certain kind-of-person performs a given role, hence is a *type*. Both individual and type relate the information that has been coded into roles to a notion of 'personality'—they are psychological, or social psychological, inferences. The last inference we can make, however, is based on the realisation that roles are related not just to abstract, neutral structures but to divisions in society, to groups that are in struggle with each other, primarily along class and gender lines but also along racial and sexual lines. In this perspective, we can see the person—or character, if we're dealing with a novel or film—as a *member* of a given class or social group.

One of the implications of this break-down is that there is no way of making sense of people, or of constructing characters, that is somehow given, natural or correct. Role, individual, type and member relate to different, wider, and politically significant ways of understanding the world—the first to a reified view of social structures as things that exist independently of human praxis, the second and third to explanations of the world in terms of personal dispositions and individual psychologies, and the fourth to an understanding of history in terms of class struggle (though I extend the traditional concept of class here to include race, gender and sex caste). Since the main focus of this article is stereotyping, I shall deal first and at greatest length with the question of type, but I also want to go on to deal with the two chief alternatives to it, individuals and members.

When discussing modes of character construction, it is I think better to use the broad term type and then to make distinctions within it. A type is any simple, vivid, memorable, easily-grasped and widely recognised characterisation in which a few traits are foregrounded and change or 'development' is kept to a minimum. Within this, however, we may make distinctions between social types, stereotypes and member types. (I leave out of account here typing from essentially earlier forms of fiction—*e.g.* archetypes and allegorical types — where the type is linked to metaphysical or moral principles rather than social or personal ones.) I shall deal with the first two now, and member types in the last section, since they are in important ways different from social and stereotypes.

The distinction between social type and stereotype I take from Orrin E. Klapp's book *Heroes, Villains and Fools.* The general aim of this book is to describe the social types prevalent in American society at the time at which Klapp was writing (pre-1962), that is to say, the range of kinds-of-people that, Klapp claims, Americans would expect to encounter in day-to-day life. Like much mainstream sociology Klapp's book is valuable not so much for what it asserts as for what it betrays about that which is 'taken for granted' in an established intellectual discourse. Klapp's distinction between a social type and a stereotype is very revealing in its implications:

> . . . stereotypes refer to things outside one's social world, whereas social types refer to things with which one is familiar; stereotypes tend to be conceived as functionless or dysfunctional (or, if functional, serving prejudice and conflict mainly), whereas social types serve the structure of society at many points.[6]

The point is not that Klapp is wrong—on the contrary, this is a very useful distinction—but that he is so unaware of the political implications of it that he does not even try to cover himself. For we have to ask—who is the 'one' referred to? and whom does the social structure itself serve? As Klapp proceeds to describe the American social types (*i.e.* those within 'one's social world'), the answer becomes clear—for nearly all his social types turn out to be white, middle-class, heterosexual and male. One might expect this to be true of the heroes, but it is also largely true of the villains and fools as well. That is to say that there are accepted, even recognised, ways of being bad or ridiculous, ways that 'belong' to 'one's social world'. And there are also ways of being bad, ridiculous and even heroic that do not 'belong'.

In other words, a system of social- and stereotypes refers to what is, as it were, within and beyond the pale of normalcy. Types are instances which indicate those who live by the rules of society (social types) and those whom the rules are designed to exclude (stereotypes). For this reason, stereotypes are also more rigid than social types. The latter are open-ended, more provisional, more flexible, to create the sense of freedom, choice, self-definition for those within the boundaries of normalcy. These boundaries themselves, however, must be clearly delineated, and so stereotypes, one of the mechanisms of boundary maintenance, are characteristically fixed, clear-cut, unalterable. You appear to choose your social type in some measure, whereas you are condemned to a stereotype. Moreover, the dramatic, ridiculous or horrific quality of stereotypes, as Paul Rock argues, serves to show how important it is to live by the rules:

It is plausible that much of the expensive drama and ritual which surround the apprehension and denunciation of the deviant are directed at maintaining the daemonic and isolated character of deviancy. Without these demonstrations, typifications would be weakened and social control would suffer correspondingly.[7]

It is not surprising then that the *genres* in which gays most often appear are horror films and comedy.

The establishment of normalcy through social- and stereotypes is one aspect of the habit of ruling groups—a habit of such enormous political consequences that we tend to think of it as far more premeditated than it actually is—to attempt to fashion the whole of society according to their own world-view, value-system, sensibility and ideology. So right is this world-view for the ruling groups, that they make it appear (as it does to them) as 'natural' and 'inevitable'—and for everyone—and, in so far as they succeed, they establish their hegemony. However, and this cannot be stressed too emphatically, hegemony is an *active* concept—it is something that must be ceaselessly built and rebuilt in the face of both implicit and explicit challenges to it. The subcultures of subordinated groups are implicit challenges to it, recuperable certainly but a nuisance, a thorn in the flesh; and the political struggles that are built within these sub-cultures are directly and explicitly about who shall have the power to fashion the world.

The establishment of hegemony through stereotyping has then two principle features which Roger Brown has termed ethnocentrism, which he defines as thinking 'of the norms of one's group as right for men [sic] everywhere', and the assumption that given social groups 'have inborn and unalterable psychological characteristics'.[8] Although Brown is writing in the context of cross-cultural and inter-racial stereotyping, what he says seems to me eminently transferable to the stereotyping of gays. Let me illustrate this from *The Killing of Sister George*.

By ethnocentrism, Brown means the application of the norms appropriate to one's own culture to that of others. Recasting this politically (within a culture rather than between cultures), we can say that in stereotyping the dominant groups apply their norms to subordinated groups, find the latter wanting, hence inadequate, inferior, sick or grotesque and hence reinforcing the dominant groups' own sense of the legitimacy of their domination. One of the modes of doing this for gays is casting gay relationships and characters in terms of heterosexual sex roles. Thus in *The Killing of Sister George*, George and Childie are very much presented as the man and woman respectively of the relationship, with George's masculinity expressed in her name, gruff voice, male clothes and by association with such icons of virility as horse brasses, pipes, beer and tweeds. However, George is not a man, and is 'therefore' inadequate to the role. Her 'masculinity' has to be asserted in set pieces of domination (shot to full dramatic hilt, with low angles, chiaroscuro lighting and menacing music), and her straining after male postures is a source of humour. *Sister George* emphasises the absence of men in the lesbian milieu, by structuring Childie and George's quarrels around the latter's fears of any man with whom Childie has dealings and by the imagery of dolls as surrogate children which are used in a cumulatively horrific way (analogous to some other horror films, including the director's [Robert Aldrich] earlier *Whatever Happened to Baby Jane?* [1962]) to suggest the grotesque sterility of a woman loving another woman (and so denying herself the chance of truly being a woman, *i.e.* a heterosexual mother).

The idea that this image of lesbianism indicates an inborn trait (hence reinforcing the idea that the way the dominant culture defines gays is the way we must always be) is enforced in *Sister George* partly through dialogue to that effect and partly through a chain of imagery linking lesbianism with the natural, bestial or low—the lingered-over *cigar-butt eating* episode, the emphasis on their relationship as founded on *physical domination* rather than affection, George's close friendship with a *prostitute* (someone who lives off her natural functions), the *descent* into the Gateways club, the important scene in a *lavatory,* the end of the film with George *mooing* to a deserted studio. The link between lesbians and animals is a strong feature of the iconography of gay women in films—they often wear furs, suede or leather (*e.g. The Haunting, Ann and Eve, Once is not Enough*), are interested in horses or dogs (*e.g. The Fox, La fiancée du pirate*), or are connected, through composition, montage or allusion, with animals (*e.g. Les biches, Lilith*, the cut from two women kissing to a back projection of a tarantula in the 'hippie' club in *Coogan's Bluff* [1969]).

What is wrong with these stereotypes is not that they are inaccurate. The implications of attacking them on that ground (one of the most common forms of attack) raise enormous problems for gay politics—first of all, it flies in the face of the actual efficacy of the hegemonic definitions enshrined in stereotypes, that is to say, gay people often believe (I did) that the stereotypes are accurate and act accordingly in line with them; and second, one of the things the stereotypes are onto is the fact that gay people do cross the gender barriers, so that many gay women do refuse to be typically 'feminine' just as many gay men refuse to be typically 'masculine' and we must beware of getting ourselves into a situation where we cannot defend, still less applaud, such sex-caste transgressions. What we should be attacking in stereotypes is the attempt of heterosexual society to define us for ourselves, in terms that inevitably fall short of the 'ideal' of heterosexuality (that is, taken to be the norm of being human), and to pass this definition off as necessary and natural. Both these simply bolster heterosexual hegemony, and the task is to develop our own alternative and challenging definitions of ourselves.

Stereotyping through iconography

In a film, one of the methods of stereotyping is through iconography. That is, films use a certain set of visual and aural signs which immediately bespeak homosexuality and connote the qualities associated, stereotypically, with it.

The opening of *The Boys in the Band* shows this very clearly. In a series of

31

brief shots or scenelets, each of the major characters in the subsequent film is introduced and their gay identity established. This can be quite subtle. For instance, while there is the 'obvious' imagery of Emory—mincing walk, accompanied by a poodle, shutting up an over-chic, over-gilded furniture store—there is also, cross cut with it, and with shots of the other 'boys', Michael going shopping. He wears a blue blazer and slacks, we do not see what he buys. It is a plain image. Except that the blazer, a sports garment, is too smart, the slacks too well pressed—the casualness of the garment type is belied by the fastidiousness of the grooming style. When he signs a cheque, at chic store Gucci's, we get a close-up of his hand, with a large, elaborate ring on it. Thus the same stereotypical connotations are present, whether obviously or mutedly, in the iconography of both Emory and Michael—over-concern with appearance, association with a 'good taste' that is just shading into decadence. The other 'boys' are similarly signalled, and although there is a range of stereotypes, nearly all of them carry this connotation of fastidiousness and concern with appearance. This observation can be extended to most gay male iconography—whether it be the emphasis on the grotesque artifices of make-up and obvious wigs (*e.g. Death in Venice*), body-building (*e.g. The Detective*), or sickliness of features, connoting not only depravity and mental illness but also the primped, unexposed face of the indoors (non-active, non-sporting) man (*e.g. The Eiger Sanction*).

Iconography is a kind of short-hand—it places a character quickly and economically. This is particularly useful for gay characters, for, short of showing physical gayness or having elaborate dialogue to establish it in the first few minutes, some means of communicating immediately that a character is gay has to be used. This of course is not a problem facing other stereotyped groups such as women or blacks (but it may include the working class), since the basis of their difference (gender, colour) shows whereas ours does not. However, while this is true, and, as I want to argue later, some kind of typing has positive value, it does seem that there may be a further ideological function to the gay iconography. Why, after all, is it felt so necessary to establish from the word go that a character is gay? The answer lies in one of the prime mechanisms of gay stereotyping, synechdoche—that is, taking the part for the whole. It is felt necessary to establish the character's gayness, because that one aspect of her or his personality is held to give you, and explain, the rest of the personality. By signalling gayness from the character's first appearance, all the character's subsequent actions and words can be understood, explained, and explained away, as those of a gay person. Moreover, it seems probable that gayness is, as a material category, far more fluid than class, gender or race—that is, most people are not either gay or non-gay, but have, to varying degrees, the capacity for both. However, this fluidity is unsettling both to the rigidity of social categorisation and to the maintenance of heterosexual hegemony. What's more, the invisibility of gayness may come creeping up on heterosexuality unawares and, fluid-like, seep into the citadel. It is therefore re-assuring to have gayness firmly categorised and kept separate from the start through a widely known iconography.

Stereotyping through structure

Stereotypes are also established by the function of the character in the film's structures (whether these be static structures, such as the way the film's world is shown to be organised, materially and ideologically, or dynamic ones, such as plot). I'd like here to look at a group of French films with lesbian characters —*Les biches, La chatte sans pudeur, Emmanuelle, La fiancée du pirate, La fille aux yeux d'or, Les garces* and *La religieuse.*⁴ Others could have been used, but I am restricting myself to films I have seen relatively recently. I suspect that the vast majority of films with lesbian characters in them are built on the structures I'm about to suggest, but that would require further work. There is no particular reason for picking a group of French films rather than, say, American or Swedish, although lesbian characters have been relatively common in French cinema since the late forties (*e.g. Quai des Orfèvres, Au royaume des cieux, Olivia, Huis clos, Thérèse Desqueyroux, La fille aux yeux d'or* etc.). There is also some polemical intent in the choice—I have deliberately made no distinction between the high-class porn of *Emmanuelle,* the critically acclaimed *auteurist* films *Les biches* and *La religieuse*, the commercial soft porn of *La chatte sans pudeur* and *Les garces*, the quasi-feminist *La fiancée du pirate*, and the chicly decadent *La fille aux yeux d'or.* The point is that lesbian stereotyping is no respecter of artistic merit or intellectual ambition. Whatever the ultimate merits of these films, in terms of lesbianism there is little to choose between them.

There is some iconographic stereotyping in these films. The chief lesbian characters are usually considerably smarter than the other female character(s) —they are often associated with the older world of *haute couture* (older in the sense both of a previous age and of being for older women), their clothes more expertly cut, their appearance always showing greater signs of thought and care, smart coiffure, use of unflashy, quality jewellery, and a taste for clothes made from animal skins. Mannish clothes are also found—jodhpurs and hacking jacket for Irène in *La fiancée du pirate*, khaki shirt and trousers for Bee in *Emmanuelle*—though this never goes so far as actually wearing men's clothes. Rather they are well coutured women's versions of men's clothing. What both types of clothing emphasise are hard, precise lines, never disguising the female form, but presenting it conspicuously without frills or fussiness or any sort of softness—in a word, without 'femininity'. (The exception here is the Mother Superior in *La religieuse*, who deliberately softens the lines of her habit with frills.) However, the full significance of this, especially as it compares to the rather dressed-down appearance of the central female protagonist, only becomes clear from a consideration of the films' structures.

In terms of the structure of the lesbian relationships as the films show them, it seems that the films always feel a need to recreate the social inequality of heterosexuality within homosexuality. By this I mean that whereas heterosexual relationships involve people defined as social unequals (or oppressor and oppressed, men and women)—an inequality that while not insuperable is always there as a problem in heterosexual relationships—homosexual relationships involve two people who, in terms of sex caste, are equals (both women or both men). Films, however, are seldom happy to acknowledge this and so introduce other forms of social inequality which are seen as having a primary role in defining the nature of the gay relationship. In the case of the films under consideration, this is done primarily through age, but with strong under-pinnings of money and class. Thus Leo (*La fille aux yeux d'or*), Elaine (*Les garces*), Bee (*Emmanuelle*), and Frédérique (*Les biches*) are older than 'the girl', Juliette, Emmanuelle and Why respectively, while Leo and Frédérique, as well as Irène (*La fiancée du pirate*) are also richer. (This of course in turn relates to the ideological connection of gayness with the idle sexual experi-mentation of the rich and the mistaken belief that there is no such thing as a working-class gay.) This inequality is more clear-cut between the Mother Superior and Suzanne in *La religieuse*. In the films under discussion, only Martina in *La chatte sans pudeur* is no older or richer than Julie. But it is clear that she, like Leo, Elaine, Bee, Frédérique, Irène and the Mother Superior, is the stronger of the lesbian pair. This is partly because she, like them, is shown to take initiative and precipitate various events in the plot; and partly be-cause, like them, she is involved in the central structure of the film, which we may characterise as a struggle for control.

This struggle is for control over the central female character. Control here means, as much as anything, definition, for what characterises these central figures is that they are without character, they are unformed. (Hence their dress is iconographically almost striking in its non-descriptness.) They are not just passive, they are nothing, an absence. Suzanne takes no decisions after her initial (defeated) stand against taking holy orders—things happen to her, people struggle to make her what they want her to be. The same negative function holds for the others. Why does not even have a name—she is just a question mark. And similarly we never get to know the name of the girl with golden eyes.

In this struggle it is the lesbian who must be defeated. The central character is sexually malleable to a degree—she will be had by anyone, not because she is voracious but because her sexuality is undefined. But defeat of the lesbian by the man signals that the true sexual definition of a woman is heterosexual and that she gets that definition from a man. This is clearest in *Emmanuelle*, where there is not so much a struggle between a lesbian and a heterosexual male protagonist as a progression for Emmanuelle from vaguely unsatisfactory marital sex through lesbianism (with Bee) to relations with Mario. (In this *Emmanuelle* is following the plot structure of very many recent soft porno-graphy films.) After her affair with Bee, Emmanuelle says 'I'm not grown up yet' (*i.e.* that relationship was not an 'adult' one), while Mario is explicitly introduced as a philosopher-tutor in sexuality. The filming further reflects this progression—where the lesbianism takes place out of doors and is suffused with light, white, the later sex scenes, presided over by Mario, are indoors, dark with patches of deep rich colours. The open air purity and simplicity of lesbianism ('pretty enough in its way', the film grants), is replaced by the dark, vibrant secrets of 'mature' sexuality.

There are variations on this structure. In *La religieuse* the opposite of lesbianism is asexuality—but that is defined and demanded by priests, and throughout the film men are seen as sources of rationality set against the various insanities of convent life. In *La fille aux yeux d'or* the lesbian gets her revenge by murdering the girl. In *Les biches*, Why herself murders Frédérique and probably Paul, who, having 'defined' her, have now both let her down. In all cases, the 'committed' lesbian (as opposed to the 'undefined' girl) is seen as a perverse rival to the man (or men), condemned for trying to do what only a man can—or should—really do, that is, define and control women.

The only exception is *La fiancée du pirate*, where Maria rejects both Irène and the men, and leaves the town. Yet despite the wonderful *élan* of the film's ending,[10] it is still based on the same structure, with the lesbian character playing the same predatory, competitive role as in the other films. In other words, even in a film of great feminist appeal, heterosexual thought and feeling structures remain intact. And the gayness is there to reinforce the sense of rightness of those structures.

Individuals

The alternative to character construction through types is often held to be the creation of 'individuals'. Indeed, in certain usages, this is what the word 'character' means—thus Robert Scholes and Robert Kellogg can remark, 'in so far as a character is a type, he [sic] is less a character'[11]

This approach to character construction derives from the novel. As Ian Watt has shown, the novel made a decisive break with previous modes of fiction—in terms of character construction, it replaced historical, mythic or archetypal personages with particular, individuated characters situated in time and space; it introduced the elements of time and memory, and with them changes of personality and consciousness of those changes. Watt argues that these developments in fiction went hand in hand with the development of 'realist' philosophy (*e.g.* Descartes, Locke), although not necessarily through any direct influence of the one on the other. Rather:

> . . . both the philosophical and the literary innovations must be seen as parallel manifestations of larger change—that vast transformation of Western civilisation since the Renaissance which has replaced the unified world picture of the Middle Ages with another very different one—one which presents us, essentially, with a developing but unplanned aggregate of particular individuals having particular experiences at particular times and at particular places.[12]

In other words, capitalism and its peculiar conception of the individual.

In the cinema, character construction in terms of individuality draws on several aspects of the medium—'invisible' photography, which places characters in a definite time and space; stars, whose particularity and real existence outside the film fiction 'guarantees' the 'uniqueness' of the characters they portray; linear narrative which permits the showing of change over time; acting and scripting traditions which signal the notion of individuality; and, very often, a deliberate 'going against' types of the kind analysed by Christine Geraghty in her article on *Alice Doesn't Live Here Any More.*[13]

All of these features are evident in such individuated characterisations as those played by Dorothea Wieck and Hertha Thiele in *Mädchen in Uniform*, Danielle Darrieux in *Olivia*, Dirk Bogarde in *Victim*, Shirley MacLaine in *The Loudest Whisper*, Peter Finch in *Sunday Bloody Sunday*, and Al Pacino in *Dog Day Afternoon*. All avoid the more 'expressionist' modes of photography available in their period (*Mädchen in Uniform*) or *genre* (*Victim, Dog Day Afternoon*). All are stars who also have a reputation for being 'actors' — *i.e.* not just embodiments of modes of being but also interpreters of roles, fixing character with nuances of gesture, attention to the details of performance etc. Personal change and consciousness of change become key elements in the narrative development — for instance, Shirley MacLaine realises that perhaps after all she did love Audrey Hepburn 'like that', and hangs herself; Dirk Bogarde accepts his gayness and resolves to fight blackmail openly in the courts. Stereotypes of gays are shown in *Victim* and *Dog Day Afternoon*, the better to distinguish Bogarde and Pacino from them. (Pacino becomes a hero for the crowd outside the bank, but the film never allows this to become identification with the painted gay activists who turn up to support him.) Going against stereotypes can also operate at the structural level—thus triangle situations like those in the French films (two people of opposite sex in love with the same person) are set up in *The Loudest Whisper* and *Sunday Bloody Sunday*, but Shirley MacLaine and Peter Finch do not fight to control the ones they love but rather insist on granting them autonomy. They even get on with their rivals—James Garner and Glenda Jackson, respectively.

There is no doubt that these performances had a progressive impact. They showed that gays are human—that is, that gays can be portrayed according to the norms of what it is to be human in this society. The problem is that these norms themselves, by their focus on uniqueness and inner growth, tend to prevent people from seeing themselves in terms of class, sex group or race. The very density, richness, refinement and 'roundness' of these characterisations, and especially the device of setting up the individual gays over against the stereotypes, make it very difficult to think of there being solidarity, sisterhood or brotherhood, collective identity and action between the gay protagonist and her/his sex caste.[14] The net result is that these films tend to stress gayness as a personality issue, a problem to which there are only individual solutions— suicide (*Mädchen in Uniform, The Loudest Whisper*), bank-robbing (*Dog Day Afternoon*), mature resignation (*Sunday Bloody Sunday*) and so on.

This does not mean that individual character construction is unable to deal with social issues, with the determinations that act on a human life. For instance, *Mädchen in Uniform*, as Janet Meyers writes, brings out:

> ... the causal connection ... between the control and repression of feelings between women and the maintenance of fascist values.[15]

Equally, *Victim* makes clear how the law operates on the lives of gay men. Yet in both cases the central articulation is still the individual versus society as a whole, not the individual as a member of an oppressed group. This becomes quite clear if one considers *Victim*, the film amongst this group which gets closest to seeing gays as oppressed—but it does that not through Bogarde, who keeps his distance from the other gays, even when he embarks on his personal crusade for law reform, but through the cross-section of gay types that are set over against him (who perhaps come close to being member types rather than stereotypes).

Member types

Member types are not, in their mode of construction (*i.e.* use of vivid, recognisable icons, lack of development etc.), different from social- and stereotypes. Where they differ is in the correlation made between the type and social reality. Social- and stereotypes are linked to psychological categories, sorts of personality, within or without a cultural hegemony. Member types, on the other hand, are linked to historically and culturally specific and determined social groups or classes and their praxes, which are almost bound to be outside the present cultural hegemony (in so far as it has so much invested in the notion of individuality).

Member types may, for now, be achieved by strategies such as more 'obvious' typing, melodrama, fantasy and montage, which, as Pam Cook writes of Dorothy Arzner's films, 'denaturalise' the stereotypes, and allow for an understanding of the concrete and ideological forces that determine them.[16] I'd like to suggest how this may happen from an account of *Some of my Best Friends Are...*

Best Friends is obviously similar to *The Boys in the Band*—a single evening in a single setting, with some claim to presenting an anatomy of male gay life. There is not much to choose between them in terms of the particular gallery of types they choose to present. But *Boys* is more subtle and individualising (*i.e.* it is a mixture of type and individual character construction). Its narrative centres on character development (*e.g.* Larry and Hank come to see more clearly the nature of the problems of their relationship and resolve to work at improving it; Alan realises he does love his wife; Michael comes face to face with his own self-disgust, and this brings out reserves of strength in the insecure Donald; and so on). By setting it in a private home and excluding non-gay characters (except Alan) and women, the drama is located in individual personalities, personal strengths and weaknesses. By using loose pacing, allowing for *longueurs* and the illusion of randomness, and eschewing non-naturalistic devices such as non-eye-level camera angles, inserts, varieties of editing rhythm and so on, it conforms to the perceptual conventions of realism. Point for point, *Best Friends* is different.

The narrative is organised around a multiplicity of strands, none of which can be developed in terms of exploration of character, and which usually come to a head in a series of melodramatic or comic set pieces—Terry's mother denouncing him, and Scott insisting he stay with him rather than go and beg her forgiveness; Cheri/Philip, realising Tom cannot accept him (because he's a man), suddenly hoisted above everyone's heads, with wings and wand, to the chant of 'We believe in fairies!'—set pieces which orchestrate, respectively, the opposed loyalties of family and sexuality, and the possibility of gay solidarity. That is to say, this organisation of types permits a certain generalising force about the gay *situation*. Particularly interesting here is the way the exaggeratedly heterosexual role-play of the hustler, fag-hag Lita and transvestite Karen (which in the case of the first two is also intended by them as a taunt to the gay characters) is exposed as factitious, inappropriate and masking profound insecurities, alongside the low key style of the couples and the freely embraced camping about of Cheri and the rest.

Where *Boys* is set in a private home, *Best Friends* is set in a gay club, which is controlled by straight society. This allows it to show the operation of oppression on the lives, life-styles (and hence life-types) of gay people. The enclosedness of *Boys* can only be seen as a function of the characters' own cliqueishness, whereas *Best Friends* shows that this banding together (with which straights often reproach gays) is a product of ghettoisation. The song, *Where Do You Go?*, and much of the dialogue, emphasises this. The economics of the ghetto—the straight owner's recognition of the club as 'a gravy train', his mock friendly relations with the police to whom he is paying protection—are clearly located in non-gay interests; and the fact that the policeman who collects the protection turns out to be the transvestite Karen's boyfriend reinforces the notion that gay people work in the interests of straight society (often against themselves). The oppressiveness of the ghetto is finally made clear by the end of the film, where our hoped-for romantic moment—Barrett coming back for Michel to commit himself to him rather than clinging on to his empty heterosexual marriage—is denied us because the straight owners cannot be bothered to open up the club for Barrett. We know Michel is inside. As they drive away, one of the barmen remarks that there is still someone in the club asleep, but they decide to leave him—'He'll still be there in the morning—where else has a faggot got to go?' Thus the control of the ghetto—by straights—is shown, schematically perhaps but chillingly too, as destructive of gay relationships.

Best Friends maintains a tight, even old-fashioned, control on the narrative, building to melodramatic climaxes and wringing all the emotion out of them. It makes free use of camera angles and composition to stress the characters' relatedness to the specific environment of the club (thereby reinforcing the notion of a social situation). Cutting in of events from the characters' pasts make connections—of tension and release, of conflicting demands—between how they are placed within the dominant straight culture and the brief, concentrated moment of gayness permitted them in ghetto life. Cut-in fantasy sequences, such as Karen's vision of herself dressed and beautiful as Lita, dancing with the hustler in tie and tails; Howard's day-dream of the club members dressed as choristers (thus reintegrating for him his gayness and his religious beliefs)—suggest the gap between aspiration and reality in gay lives.

In all these ways then *Some of My Best Friends Are . . .* suggests the possibility of a mode of representation that does not dissolve concrete social distinctions into psychologistic ones (whether these be individualised or social/stereotypical), but emphasises such distinctions as the basis of collective identity and the heart of historical struggle. It would be absurd to maintain that *Best Friends* actually achieved this (and much more so that it was consciously aiming to). And there is the additional problem that we are brought up to 'read' types in the psychologistic ways I've suggested, so that it is doubtful if the majority of cinema-goers would actually construct from *Best Friends* the kind of anatomy of ghetto oppression that I've just done. What I hope to have brought out, however, is the importance of holding on to some concept of typing (in the way we make films, as producers or audience) at the same time as we are exposing the reactionary political force of most social and stereo-typing.

Notes

1. See Ken Plummer, *Sexual Stigma*, Tavistock, London, 1974.
2. The concept of self-oppression is crucial to an understanding of the politics of homosexuality. It is excellently examined in Andrew Hodges and David Hutter, *With Downcast Gays,* Pomegranate Press, London, 1974.
3. *E.g.* Jim Pines, *Blacks in Films*, Studio Vista, London, 1975; Claire Johnston (ed.), *Notes on Women's Cinema*, SEFT, London, 1973.
4. Classic texts in this area include G. H. Mead, *Mind, Self and Society*, University of Chicago Press, 1934; Alfred Schutz in M. Natanson (ed.), *Collected Papers*, Martinus Nijhoff, The Hague, 1967; Peter Berger and Thomas Luckman, *The Social Construction of Reality*, Allen Lane, London, 1967; Talcott Parsons, *The Social System*, Free Press, New York, 1951; Elizabeth Burns, *Theatricality*, Longman, London, 1972. The terminology used is my own.
5. A view stemming ultimately from Durkheim but detectable in most mainstream sociology.
6. Orrin E. Klapp, *Heroes, Villains and Fools*, Prentice-Hall, Englewood Cliffs, 1962, p. 16.
7. Paul Rock, *Deviant Behaviour*, Hutchinson, London, 1973, pp. 34-5.
8. Roger Brown, *Social Psychology*, Macmillan, New York & London, 1965, p. 183.
9. *La chatte sans pudeur* and *Les garces* were distributed in this country with the titles *Sexy Lovers* and *Love Hungry Girls* respectively.
10. The ending of *La fiancée* is a problem, I think. She is probably on her way to join a man who runs a travelling cinema; one of the films he shows, a poster for which she passes on her way out of the village, has the same title as the film we are watching. In a sense then, his film defines her . . .
11. Robert Scholes and Robert Kellogg, *The Nature of Narrative*, OUP, Oxford, 1966, p.204.
12. Ian Watt, *The Rise of the Novel*, Penguin, 1963, p.32.
13. Christine Geraghty, *'Alice Doesn't Live Here Any More'*, *Movie* (London), No. 22, pp.39-42.
14. This is perhaps further enforced by the fact that the stars playing the parts are assumed not to be gay—or were when the film was made.
15. Janet Meyers, 'Dyke Goes to the Movies', *Dyke* (New York), Spring 1976, p. 38.
16. Pam Cook, 'Approaching the work of Dorothy Arzner', in Claire Johnston (ed.), *The Work of Dorothy Arzner*, BFI, London, 1974.

Camp and the gay sensibility

by Jack Babuscio

What I aim to do in this essay is to consider some of the ways in which individual films, stars and directors reflect a gay sensibility. In the course of this exploration, I hope to accomplish the following aims: to provide a more precise definition of what is, at present, a most confused area of response that goes under the vague label of *camp*; to ascertain the relationship of camp and gayness; to consider some of the social patterns and mechanisms that make for the gay sensibility; to relate these considerations to cinema with the purpose of stimulating discussion of a hitherto neglected aspect of film; to promote solidarity and a greater sense of identification among gays; to remind readers of the fact that what we see in cinema is neither truth nor reality, but fabrications: individual, subjective perceptions of the world and its inhabitants; and, finally, to argue that there is far more fun in art and art in fun than many of us will even now allow.

The gay sensibility

I define the gay sensibility as a creative energy reflecting a consciousness that is different from the mainstream; a heightened awareness of certain human complications of feeling that spring from the fact of social oppression; in short, a perception of the world which is coloured, shaped, directed and defined by the fact of one's gayness. Such a perception of the world varies with time and place according to the nature of the specific set of circumstances in which, historically, we have found ourselves. Present-day society defines people as falling into distinct types. Such a method of labelling ensures that individual types become polarised. A complement of attributes thought to be 'natural' and 'normal' for members of these categories is assigned. Hence, heterosexuality = normal, natural, healthy behaviour; homosexuality = abnormal, unnatural, sick behaviour. Out of this process of polarisation there develops a twin set of perspectives and general understandings about what the world is like and how to deal with it. For gays, one such response is camp.

Camp

The term *camp* describes those elements in a person, situation or activity which express, or are created by, a gay sensibility. Camp is never a thing or person *per se*, but, rather, a relationship between activities, individuals, situations *and* gayness. People who have camp, *e.g.* screen 'personalities' such as Tallulah Bankhead or Edward Everett Horton, or who are in some way responsible for camp—Busby Berkeley or Josef von Sternberg—need not be gay. The link with gayness is established when the camp aspect of an individual or thing is identified as such by a gay sensibility. This is not to say that all gays respond in equal measure to camp, or, even, that an absolute consensus could easily be reached within our community about what to include or emphasise. Yet though camp resides largely in the eye of the beholder, there remains an underlying unity of perspective among gays that gives to someone or something its characteristic camp flavour. Four features are basic to camp: irony, aestheticism, theatricality and humour.

Camp/irony
Irony is the subject matter of camp, and refers here to any highly incongruous contrast between an individual or thing and its context or association. The most common of incongruous contrasts is that of masculine/feminine. Some of the best examples of this can be found in the screen personalities of stars whose attraction, as camp, owes much to their androgynous qualities, *e.g.* Greta Garbo in all her films, but particularly *Queen Christina* (1933), where she masquerades as a man; Mick Jagger in *Performance,* where the pop star's persona is achieved through radical neutering via the elision of masculine/feminine 'signs'; the Andy Warhol stars Holly Woodlawn, Candy Darling and Jackie Curtis in films such as *Flesh* and *Women in Revolt* (1972).

Another incongruous contrast is that of youth/(old) age: the Gloria Swanson-William Holden relationship in *Sunset Boulevard* (1950), or that of Bud Cort-Ruth Gordon in *Harold and Maude* (1971); as well as the Bette Davis characters Fanny Trellis and Jane Hudson in *Mr. Skeffington* (1944) and *Whatever Happened to Baby Jane?* (1962): aging, egocentric women obsessed with the romantic illusions of youth and unable to reconcile themselves to the reality of old age.

Other, less frequently employed contrasts are the sacred/profane (*The Picture of Dorian Gray* [1945]), spirit/flesh (*Summer and Smoke* [1961], *The Roman Spring of Mrs. Stone* [1961]), and high/low status, as in dozens of rags-to-riches musicals (*The Countess of Monte Cristo* [1934]) and melodramas (*Ruby Gentry* [1952]).

At the core of this perception of incongruity is the idea of gayness as a moral deviation. Two men or two women in love is generally regarded by society as incongruous—out of keeping with the 'normal', 'natural', 'healthy' order of things. In sum, it is thought to be morally wrong.

Camp/aestheticism
The aesthetic element is also basic to camp. Irony, if it is to be effective,

must be shaped. The art of camp therefore relies largely upon arrangement, timing and tone. Similarly, the ironic events and situations which life itself presents will be more or less effective depending on how well the precision, balance and economy of a thing is maintained. Camp is aesthetic in three inter-related ways: as a view of art; a view of life; and as a practical tendency in things or persons:

> It is through Art, and through Art only, that we can shield ourselves from the sordid perils of actual existence. [1]

Wilde's epigram points to a crucial aspect of camp aestheticism: its opposition to puritan morality. Camp is subversive of commonly received standards. As Susan Sontag has said, there is something profoundly 'propagandistic' about it:

> homosexuals have pinned their integration into society on promoting the aesthetic sense. Camp is a solvent of morality. It neutralises moral indignation. [2]

Consistently followed as a comprehensive attitude, aestheticism inevitably leads to an ingrown selfishness in life, and to triviality in art. [3] As a means to personal liberation through the exploration of experience, camp is an assertion of one's self-integrity—a temporary means of accommodation with society in which art becomes, at one and the same time, an intense mode of individualism and a form of spirited protest. And while camp advocates the dissolution of hard and inflexible moral rules, it pleads, too, for a morality of sympathy. Its viewpoint suggests detachment from conventional standards. Here again, as R. V. Johnson has pointed out, there is an aspect of aestheticism which diverges from 'a puritan ethic of rigid "thou shalt nots"', preferring, instead, to regard people and ideas with due consideration to circumstances and individual temperament. [4]

A good example of this is found in Jack Hazan's quasi-documentary portrait of artist David Hockney, *A Bigger Splash*. Here the director manages to convey the wry, distancing nature of his subject's visual humour as an integral part of a gay sensibility that is defiantly different from the mainstream. Because Hockney responds to his gay 'stigma' by challenging social and aesthetic conventions in life and art, Hazan's concern is to show the various ways in which his subject's private life affects his art—or how art records personal experience and determines our future. Thus, the film relates to the artist's work in much the same way as the paintings do to life. The presence of the unseen beneath the surface is no less important than what one actually sees.

This double aspect in which things can be taken is further emphasised by the semi-documentary nature of Hazan's film. Hockney and his friends appear as themselves, so that the relationships portrayed are much the same as in reality. But the reality is also rehearsed: Hazan occasionally suggests themes for his 'characters' to act out, and the line separating being and role-playing becomes blurred. This convention appears to suit Hockney, whose deceptive innocence and disorientating self-created face (platinum blonde hair, owl-rimmed spectacles) exhibit a special feeling for performance and a flair for the theatrical. And though the film remains, in the final analysis, a subjective record of *one* gay life in which the conjunction of fantasy and experience make common cause, it does effectively isolate the strong strain of protest that resides in the gay sensibility. By wit, a well-organised evasiveness, and a preference for the artificial, Hockney manages a breakthrough into creativity.

This detached attitude does not necessarily indicate an inability to feel or perceive the seriousness of life. In Hockney's case, it is a means of defiance: a refusal to be overwhelmed by unfavourable odds. When the world is a rejecting place, the need grows correspondingly strong to project one's being—to explore the limits to which one's personality might attain—as a way of shielding the inner self from those on the outside who are too insensitive to understand. It is also a method whereby one can multiply personalities, play various parts, assume a variety of roles—both for fun, as well as out of real need.

In film, the aesthetic element in camp further implies a movement away from contemporary concerns into realms of exotic or subjective fantasies; the depiction of states of mind that are (in terms of commonly accepted taboos and standards) suspect; an emphasis on sensuous surfaces, textures, imagery and the evocation of mood as stylistic devices—not simply because they are appropriate to the plot, but as fascinating in themselves. Such tendencies as these are consonant with the spirit of aestheticism in camp, and also go some way towards explaining the charm which particular film *genres* have for a certain section of our community.

The horror *genre,* in particular, is susceptible to a camp interpretation. Not all horror films are camp, of course; only those which make the most of stylish conventions for expressing instant feeling, thrills, sharply defined personality, outrageous and 'unacceptable' sentiments, and so on. In addition, the psychological issues stated or implied, along with the sources of horror, must relate to some significant aspect of our situation and experience; *e.g.* the inner drives which threaten an individual's well-being and way of life (Tourneur's *The Cat People* [1942], Mamoulian's *Dr. Jekyll and Mr. Hyde* [1941]), coping with pressures to conform and adapt (Siegel's *Invasion of the Body Snatchers* [1956]), the masking of 'abnormality' behind a façade of 'normality' (Robson's *The Seventh Victim* [1943], Ulmer's *The Black Cat* [1943]), personal rebellion against enforced restrictions (Burrowe's *Incense for the Damned* [1970]).

As a practical tendency in things or persons, camp emphasises style as a means of self-projection, a conveyor of meaning and an expression of emotional tone. Style is a form of consciousness; it is never 'natural', always acquired. Camp is also urban; it is, in part, a reaction to the anonymity, boredom and socialising tendencies of technological society.

Camp aims to transform the ordinary into something more spectacular. In terms of style, it signifies performance rather than existence. Clothes and décor, for example, can be a means of asserting one's identity, as well as a form of justification in a society which denies one's essential validity. [5] Just as the dandy of the nineteenth century sought in material visibility (as Auden has said of Baudelaire) 'a way out of the corrupt nature into which he, like everyone else, is born'[6], so many in our community find in the decorative arts and the cultivation of exquisite taste a means of making something positive from a discredited social identity. Hence, the *soigné* furniture and furnishings of the flat designed for Franz in Fassbinder's *Fox and his Friends*, or the carefully cluttered modishness of Michael's apartment in William Friedkin's film adaptation of Mart Crowley's *The Boys in the Band*. *

By such means as these one aims to become what one wills, to exercise some control over one's environment. But the emphasis on style goes further. Camp is often exaggerated. When the stress on style is 'outrageous' or 'too much', it results in incongruities: the emphasis shifts from what a thing or a person *is* to what it *looks* like; from *what* is being done to *how* it is being done.

This stress on stylisation can also explain why the musical comedy, with its high budgets and big stars, its open indulgence in sentiment, and its emphasis on atmosphere, mood, nostalgia and the fantastic, is, along with horror, a film *genre* that is saturated with camp. This can best be seen in the boldly imaginative production numbers of Busby Berkeley, whose work reveals a penchant for total extravagance, voyeurism and sexual symbolism that is particularly blatant in 'The Lady in the Tutti-Frutti Hat' sequence of *The Girls He Left Behind* [1943] (also called *The Gang's All Here*), with its acres of female flesh, outrageously phallic dancing bananas, and Carmen Miranda at her most aggressively self-assertive.

Camp/theatricality

The third element of camp is theatricality. To appreciate camp in things or persons is to perceive the notion of life-as-theatre, being versus role-playing, reality and appearance. If 'role' is defined as the appropriate behaviour associated with a given position in society, then gays do not conform to socially expected ways of behaving as men and women. Camp, by focusing on the outward appearances of role, implies that roles, and, in particular, sex roles, are superficial—a matter of style. Indeed, life itself is role and theatre, appearance and impersonation.

*A distinction must be drawn here between kitsch and camp. The latter implies fervent involvement—an ability to strongly identify with what is perceived as camp. Not so the former, which refers to the artistically shallow or vulgar, and is marked by sensationalism, sentimentalism and slickness. With regard to décor, kitsch can be seen in George Schlatter's *Norman . . . Is That You?*, where the furniture, curtains, chandeliers, paintings, ornaments, etc. provided by set decorator Fred R. Price function principally as things to be mocked.

Theatricality relates to the gay situation primarily in respect to roles. Gays do not conform to sex-role expectations: we do not show appropriate interest in the opposite sex as a possible source of sexual satisfaction. We are therefore seen as something less than 'real' men and women. This is the essence of gay stigma, our so-called 'failing'. Gayness is seen as a sort of collective denial of the moral and social order of things. Our very lifestyle indicates a rejection of that most cherished cultural assumption which says that masculinity (including sexual dominance over women) is 'natural' and appropriate for men, and femininity (including sexual submissiveness towards men) is 'natural' and appropriate for women. The stigma of gayness is unique insofar as it is not immediately apparent either to ourselves or to others. Upon discovery of our gayness, however, we are confronted with the possibility of avoiding the negative sanctions attached to our supposed failing by concealing information (*i.e.* signs which other people take for gay) from the rest of the world. This crucial fact of our existence is called *passing for straight*, a phenomenon generally defined in the metaphor of theatre, that is, playing a role: pretending to be something that one is not; or, to shift the motive somewhat, to camouflage our gayness by withholding facts about ourselves which might lead others to the correct conclusion about our sexual orientation.[7]

The art of passing is an acting art: to pass is to be 'on stage', to impersonate heterosexual citizenry, to pretend to be a 'real' (*i.e.* straight) man or woman. Such a practice of passing (which can be occasional, continuous, in the past or present) means, in effect, that one must be always on one's guard lest one be seen to 'deviate' from those culturally standardised canons of taste, behaviour, speech, etc. that are generally associated with the male and female roles as defined by the society in which we live. Because masculinity and femininity are perceived in exclusively heterosexual terms, our social stereotype (and often, self-image) is that of one who rejects his or her masculinity or femininity. Those unwilling to accept their socially defined roles are appropriately stigmatised. Proving one's 'manhood' or being a 'lady' is thus closely linked to the rejection of gay characteristics. In women, repression is often internalised; in men, it may be externalised in aggressive behaviour.

The experience of passing is often productive of a gay sensibility. It can, and often does, lead to a heightened awareness and appreciation for disguise, impersonation, the projection of personality, and the distinctions to be made between instinctive and theatrical behaviour. The experience of passing would appear to explain the enthusiasm of so many in our community for certain stars whose performances are highly charged with exaggerated (usually sexual) role-playing. Some of these seem (or are made to seem) fairly 'knowing', if not self-parodying, in their roles: Jayne Mansfield holding two full milk bottles to her breasts in *The Girl Can't Help It* (1957); Bette Davis in *Beyond the Forest* (1949); Anita Ekberg in *La dolce vita*; Mae West in all her films; Cesar Romero as the Cisco Kid and in *The Good Fairy* (1935). Others are apparently more 'innocent' or 'sincere': Jane Russell in *The Outlaw* (1943); Raquel Welch; Mamie van Doren; Jennifer Jones in *Duel in the Sun* (1947); Johnny Weismuller as Tarzan and Jungle Jim; Ramon Novarro, particularly in *Ben Hur* (1927) and *The Student Prince (in Old Heidelberg)* [1928].

The time factor is also crucial to one's appreciation of camp theatricality. A good deal of the screen acting which only recently appeared quite 'natural' will, in the goodness of time, doubtless become camp for its high degree of stylisation (that is, if it is not already camp). Examples: the 'method' acting of Rod Steiger and early Brando; so, too, the charming, 'dated' styles of George Arliss, Luise Rainer or Miriam Hopkins. Similarly, a number of personalities from the silent cinema, once revered for their sexual allure, now seem, in the seventies, fairly fantastic: Theda Bara and Pola Negri. Men, as David Thomson has observed, have always had an insecure hold on the camera,[8] so that male sex appeal, *e.g.* in the case of Rudolph Valentino, vanished much more quickly than did the sway exerted by women. Finding such stars camp is not to mock them, however. It is more a way of poking fun at the whole cosmology of restrictive sex roles and sexual identifications which our society uses to oppress its women and repress its men—including those on screen. This is not to say that those who appreciate the camp in such stars must, *ipso facto*, be politically 'aware'; often, they are not. The response is mainly instinctive; there is something of the shock of recognition in it—the idea of seeing on screen the absurdity of those roles that each of us is urged to play with such a deadly seriousness.

Thus, camp as a response to performance springs from the gay sensibility's preference for the *intensities* of character, as opposed to its content: what the character conveys tends to be less important than *how* or *why* it is conveyed. Camp is individualistic; as such, it relishes the uniqueness and the force with which personality is imbued. This theatricalisation of experience derives both from the passing experience (wherein, paradoxically, we learn the value of the self while at the same time rejecting it) and from a heightened sensitivity to aspects of a performance which others are likely to regard as routine or uncalculated.[9] It is this awareness of the double aspect of a performance that goes a long way to explain why gays form a disproportionately large and enthusiastic part of the audience of such stars as, most notably, Judy Garland.

In part, at least, Garland's popularity owes much to the fact that she is always, and most intensely, herself. Allied to this is the fact that many of us seem able to equate our own strongly-felt sense of oppression (past or present) with the suffering/loneliness/misfortunes of the star both on and off the screen. Something in the star's personality allows for an empathy that colours one's whole response to the performer and the performance. As Vicki Lester in Cukor's *A Star is Born* (1954), but, especially, as the concert singer in Ronald Neame's *I Could Go on Singing* (1962), Garland took on roles so disconcertingly close to her real-life situation and personality that the autobiographical connections actually appeared to take their toll on her physical appearance from one scene to the next. Such performances as these solidified the impression, already formed in the minds of her more ardent admirers, of an integrity arising directly from out of her great personal misfortunes.

Camp/humour

The fourth characteristic of camp is its humour. This results from an identification of a strong incongruity between an object, person or situation and its context. The comic element is inherent in the formal properties of irony. There is a basic contradiction or incongruity, coupled with a real or pretended innocence. But in order for an incongruous contrast to be ironic it must, in addition to being comic, affect one as 'painful'—though not so painful as to neutralise the humour. It is sufficient that sympathy is aroused for the person, thing or idea that constitutes the target of an incongruous contrast. To be affected in this way, one's feelings need to clash. It follows, then, that—as A. R. Thompson has argued in his study of irony:

> contrasts which conform exactly to the objective definitions of irony are not ironical at all when they do not arouse . . . conflicting feelings.[10]

Humour constitutes the strategy of camp: a means of dealing with a hostile environment and, in the process, of defining a positive identity. This humour takes several forms. Chief of these is bitter-wit, which expresses an underlying hostility and fear. Society says to gays (and to all stigmatised groups) that we are members of the wider community; we are subject to the same laws as 'normals'; we must pay our taxes, etc.; we are, in short, 'just like everybody else'. On the other hand, we are not received into society on equal terms; indeed, we are told that we are unacceptably 'different' in ways that are absolutely fundamental to our sense of self and social identity. In other words, the message conveyed to us by society is highly contradictory: we are just like everyone else, and yet . . . we are not. It is this basic contradiction, this joke, that has traditionally been our destiny.

Not surprisingly, this contradiction has produced, in many, an identity-ambivalence that has found expression in our talk, our behaviour, our artistic efforts; in fact, our whole perception of the world and of our place in it. Like other oppressed groups, gays have developed skills out of much the same need to concentrate on strategy when the rules are stacked against us. Those of us who are sufficiently sensitive to criticism of ourselves may develop a commensurate ability to isolate, dissect, and bring into vivid focus the destructiveness and hypocrisy of others. It is thus that in much of our humour lies a strain of irony that is strongly flavoured with hostility for society, as well as for ourselves. As Erving Goffman has said:

> Given that the stigmatised individual in our society acquires identity standards which he applies to himself in spite of failing to conform to

them, it is inevitable that he will feel some ambivalence about his own self.[11]

This tendency to see ourselves as others do is to some extent changing, and will continue to change as we come to define ourselves in terms that do not assume heterosexuality as the norm. In the past, however, and, to a lesser extent, in the present, our response to this split between heterosexual standards and self-demands has been a bitter-wit that is deeply imbued with self-hate and self-derogation. This can best be illustrated in films such as *Staircase, Boys in the Band* and *The Killing of Sister George,* all of which are perhaps far too maudlin to be called camp, but whose characters do reflect, in exaggerated form, much of that bitter-wit that goes by the name of camp.

For example, in *Staircase,* directed by Stanley Donen, the humour is saturated with the sadness of those perceived as doomed to live their lives with 'unsuitable' emotions in a world where such feelings are tacitly recognised but officially condemned. Thus, throughout the film, the dialogue comments on the central couple's awful-funny confrontation with the 'normal' world outside; it is riddled with the self-hatred and low self-esteem of those who have successfully internalised straight society's opinion of us. Self-pity and an aching sense of loss are the prevailing themes: 'You've been a father,' Charlie hisses at Harry, 'a privilege denied thousands of us!' Such dialogue, geared for a 'superior' laugh, is squarely based on the tacit acceptance of the hegemony of heterosexual institutions. As for Donen's own patronising view of these proceedings, this finds its most appropriate metaphor in the maudlin tones of Ray Charles pleading in song on the soundtrack over the flickering images of gay *angst* to 'Forgive them for they know not what they do'. Finally, the very conventions of the commercial cinema provide their own language of lament via the presence of such big-name, belligerently straight-associated types as Rex Harrison (Charlie) and Richard Burton (Harry).

Camp can thus be a means of undercutting rage by its derision of concentrated bitterness. Its vision of the world is comic. Laughter, rather than tears, is its chosen means of dealing with the painfully incongruous situation of gays in society. Yet it is also true that camp is something of a proto-political phenomenon. It assumes gayness to be a category that defines the self, and it steadfastly refuses to repudiate our long heritage of gay ghetto life. Any appreciation of camp, therefore, expresses an empathy with typical gay experiences, even when this takes the form of finding beauty in the seemingly bizarre and outrageous, or discovering the worthiness in a thing or person that is supposedly without value. Finally, camp can be subversive—a means of illustrating those cultural ambiguities and contradictions that oppress us all, gay and straight, and, in particular, women.

Yet because camp combines fun and earnestness, it runs the risk of being considered not serious at all. Usually overlooked by critics of the gay sensibility is camp's strategy of irony. Camp, through its introduction of style, aestheticism, humour and theatricality, allows us to witness 'serious' issues with temporary detachment, so that only later, after the event, are we struck by the emotional and moral implications of what we have almost passively absorbed. The 'serious' is, in fact, crucial to camp. Though camp mocks the solemnities of our culture, it never totally discards the seriousness of a thing or individual. As a character in a Christopher Isherwood novel says:

> You can't camp about something you don't take seriously; you're not making fun *of* it; you're making fun *out* of it. You're expressing what's basically serious to you in terms of fun and artifice and elegance.[12]

Camp and the serious: Fassbinder's *Bitter Tears*

As a way of illustrating camp in service of the serious, consider Rainer Werner Fassbinder's *The Bitter Tears of Petra von Kant*. Here, as in almost all of this director's work, the problem of how to make radical social commentary without alienating audiences is resolved by distancing the action—finding a common denominator to anchor the message'. In *Bitter Tears* the mannerist stylisation which dominates the *mise en scène*, the grand gestures, comic routines, and the melodramatic tendencies of the plot, constitute the strategy whereby Fassbinder aims to both distance and engage his audience. As Thomas Elsaesser has pointed out in 'A Cinema of Vicious Circles', Fassbinder's search for an 'unprovocative realism' has led the director to discover for the German cinema 'the importance of being artificial' as a strategy for forcing an audience to question its assumptions about society and its inhabitants.[13]

This artificiality is the camp aspect of *Bitter Tears*. A highly theatricalised world devoid of the very passions that constitute its subject is provided by the director's formalised, almost Racinian dialogue; his elaborate, carefully calculated compositions locked into theatrical tableaux; the anachronistic costumes and mask-like makeup that reflect the psychological situation of the characters; the comic pop/classical music references—the incongruous juxtaposition of Verdi, the Platters, and the Walker Brothers; the stylised performances and ritualised division of the film into five acts, each heralded by the heroine's change of dress and wig; the expressive lighting effects that emphasise a world of masters and servants, predators and victims; and, generally, the formalised editing style which makes the most of the film's single set—a studio apartment that is dominated by a huge brass bed, a wall-sized mural-with-male-nude that bears ironic witness to the action below, and a scattered group of bald-pated mannequins whose poses are continuously rearranged as commentary on their human counterparts.

Each scene is so organised as to heighten the irony of Petra von Kant's (Margit Carstensen) inability to reconcile theory (a loving relationship must be free, honest and non-possessive) and practice. This failure is particularly apparent in Petra's sado-masochistic relationship with the omnipresent Marlene (Irm Hermann), a silent witness to her mistress's jealous possession of the sensual young model Karen (Hanna Schygulla), who ultimately rejects her benefactress in favour of her (Karen's) former husband. When, in the bitterly ironic final scene, an outrageous mixture of comedy and cruelty, the chastened Petra reverses roles and offers 'freedom and joy' to Marlene in return for companionship, the chalk-faced 'slave' dispassionately packs her bags and makes a hasty exit, pausing only to drop 'The Great Pretender' on the gramophone by way of vocal reply.

It is the very artificiality of Fassbinder's *Bitter Tears* which serves to support the characters and their emotions. The camp aspect of the work emerges in the use of calculated melodrama and flamboyant visual surfaces to accentuate the film's complex of interrelated themes: the interdependence of sex and power, love and suffering, pleasure and pain; the lover's demand for exclusive possession, which springs from vanity; the basic instability of love in the absence of a lover's sense of positive self-identity; the value of pose as an escape and protective shield; the inevitability of inequities within relationships so long as love, ego, or insights are distributed in unequal proportions. Such themes as these carry a special resonance for the gay sensibility. As outsiders, we are forced to create our own norms; to impose our *selves* upon a world which refuses to confront the arbitrariness of cultural conventions that insist on sexual loyalty, permanence and exclusive possession. Fassbinder's film, by paying close attention to the ironic functions of style, aims to detach us, temporarily, from the serious content of the images—but which, later, encourages a more reflective analysis.

Further studies of the gay sensibility in relation to cinema will need to take account of the interaction of camp and *genres, auteur* theory, images of women, etc. What follows are two brief, tentative case studies concerning camp and the gay sensibility in relation to the work of a single director (Josef von Sternberg) and in various films based on the drama and fiction of Tennessee Williams.

Sternberg as camp

To explain the relation of Sternberg to camp it is necessary to return, briefly, to the phenomenon of passing for straight. This strategy of survival in a hostile world has sensitised us to disguises, impersonations, the significance of surfaces, the need to project personality, the intensities of character, etc. Sternberg's films—in particular, the Dietrich films from *Morocco* (1930) to *The Devil is a Woman* (1935)—are all camp insofar as they relate to those adjustment mechanisms of the gay sensibility. But they are also camp in that they reflect the director's ironic attitude towards his subject-matter—a judgment which says, in effect, that the content is of interest only insofar as it remains susceptible to transformation by means of stylisation. What counts in one's view of Sternberg's films as camp, then, is the perception of an underlying emotonal autobiography—a disguise of self and obsessions by means of the artificial. One does not need to see these disguises in a strictly literal way. It is enough to sense the irony in the tensions that arise from Sternberg's anguish and cynicism, and his predilection for the most outrageous sexual symbolism as a means of objectifying personal fantasies.

Those who view camp either as a trivialisation of taste or a cultural conspiracy will frown on any labelling of Sternberg as camp. Indeed, several of this director's staunchest admirers have already attempted to 'rescue' him from ridicule and replace his reputation in a suitably dignified light.[14] For such critics neither the total experience nor the attitudes and emotional philosophy of the sensibility that produces camp are to be taken seriously. The validity of the camp statement, along with its cultural origins and associations, are regarded as of scant significance. Totally ignored is the fact that camp takes a radically different approach to the serious, one which relies heavily on aesthetic rather than moral considerations. Thus, to find camp in Sternberg is not to surrender to the joys of 'over-decorated "aesthetic" nothings'.[15] It is, rather, to appreciate the wit by which Sternberg renders his insights artificial; to sense something of an 'affaire' between Dietrich and her director; to perceive the deep significance of appearances—a sumptuous surface that serves not as an empty and meaningless background, but as the very subject of the films: a visual context for Sternberg's fantasies.

Sternberg's style is the inevitable result of his need to impose himself upon his material; to control all the elements with which creative work concerns itself. Self-revelation is best accomplished when viewers are left undistracted by the story line. The more hackneyed the material, the better the opportunities for self-projection. There is no place for spontaneity in such a scheme, as one needs always to be in total control of the information conveyed by camera, sets, actors, etc. Thus, the director demanded complete domination over every aspect of his films. His pictures were 'acts of arrogance'.[16] Not only did the act of creation derive from him, but he, Sternberg, was also the object created: 'Marlene is not Marlene,' he insisted, 'she is me.'[17]

Claire Johnston has said of *Morocco* that

in order for a man to remain at the centre of the universe in a text which focuses on the image, the *auteur* is forced to repress the idea of woman as a social and sexual being (her Otherness) and to deny the opposition man/woman altogether. The woman as sign, then, becomes the pseudo-centre of the filmic discourse.

The incongruous contrast posed by the sign is 'male/non-male', which the director established by disguising Dietrich in men's clothing.[18] This is a masquerade which connects with the theme of sexual ambivalence, of central concern to the gay sensibility, and recurrent in Sternberg's work. Dietrich, then, functions principally as a primary motif. It is she, woman, who becomes the focus of Sternberg's symbolism, psychology and sense of humour. As Amy Joly in *Morocco*; X-27, prostitute and spy, in *Dishonoured* (1931); Shanghai Lily, prostitute, in *Shanghai Express* (1932); Helen Faraday, nightclub entertainer and archetypal mother in *Blonde Venus* (1932); Sophia Frederica, later Catherine II, in *The Scarlet Empress* (1934); and Concha Perez in *The Devil is a Woman* (1935), Dietrich as woman becomes a manifestation of Sternberg's fantasies. The man takes over; the woman recedes into myth and the details of the décor. The image that emerges is man-made. But it is also an integral part of the larger camp structure. Hence, the danger to which camp enthusiasts expose themselves is as inevitable as it is irreducible, *i.e.* the danger of surrendering to the corroboration of Sternberg's fantasies as each, in turn, is thrown back on us by the male-manufactured image of the star who illuminates the screen.

The gay sensibility in the films of Tennessee Williams

In the films based on the work of Tennessee Williams (I shall refer to these as 'Williams's films' since, even when the plays and fiction are adapted for the screen by someone other than the author, they retain the spirit of the original) the image of women is again of central concern in any consideration of camp and the gay sensibility.[19] The point I wish to take up here is one which various critics have used to denigrate both Williams's films and the gay sensibility; namely, that the typical heroine of these films is a 'drag queen'.[20]

This interpretation is nowhere more relentlessly pursued than in Molly Haskell's *From Reverence to Rape: The Treatment of Women in the Movies*. Haskell perceives Williams's women as products of the writer's own 'baroquely transvestised homosexual fantasies'. By no stretch of the imagination, she argues, can they conceivably be seen as 'real' women. Hence, Vivien Leigh's Blanche DuBois and Karen Stone in *A Streetcar Named Desire* (1951) and *The Roman Spring of Mrs. Stone* (1961); Geraldine Page's Alexandra Del Lago (the Princess Kosmonopolis) and Alma Winemiller in *Sweet Bird of Youth* (1962) and *Summer and Smoke* (1958); Joanne Woodward's Carole Cutrere in *The Fugitive Kind* (1958); Ava Gardner's Maxine Faulk and Deborah Kerr's Hannah Jelkes in *The Night of the Iguana* (1964); Elizabeth Taylor's Flora (Sissy) Goforth in *Boom!* (1968), etc., etc. All these characters, Haskell argues, are 'hermaphrodites' who flow from out of 'the palpable fear and self-pity, guts and bravura of the aging homosexual'. What happens here, the argument further goes, is that the gay author, seething with repressed desires, dons his female mask (Blanche, Karen, etc) and hungrily heads, in print as on screen, for a host of fantasy·males of his own creation: Stanley Kowalski/Marlon Brando, Paolo/Warren Beatty, Chance Wayne/

Paul Newman, etc. The 'cultured homosexual' (Williams) is thus seen as being compelled, 'often masochistically and against his taste', to love brutes and beachboys, natives and gigolos, primitives and peasants—as well as all the other unavailable prototypes of uninhibited sensuality.[21]

There is some truth in all this, of course. Williams has 'used' women to his own advantage. His initial passing strategy for coping with the fact of his gayness was productive of deep anxiety which led to a certain conservatism in his work: a desire to protect himself against the prying eyes of others; an unwillingness to parade his feelings as a gay man in public. Thus, in films based on such early work as *A Streetcar Named Desire, Summer and Smoke* and *The Roman Spring of Mrs. Stone,* Williams's crypto-gayness found relief in the form of female guise: Blanche, Alma, Karen. These characters do express their creator's own 'unacceptable' emotions as a gay man. They all do declare the nature of Williams's own fantasy life at the time of their creation. In them the artist has found a means of dealing with the tensions that plagued and defined him—tensions that reside in such dualities as flesh/spirit, promiscuity/pride, youth/(old) age.

Yet it is also true that such a strategy of survival in a hostile world constitutes an imaginative act of which any artist is capable. Most male artists, whatever their sexual orientation, assume the habit of it as a necessary qualification in dealing with female emotions. What one needs to be concerned about is not the *fact* of an artist's fantasies; but, rather, the way in which these fantasies are *shaped* so that they speak to and for other people.

Still, there remains the threat from certain critical quarters to reduce the whole of such problems of interpretation to generalities about the limitations of the gay artist. The central assumption of such criticism is that gays, generally, can know little of life as lived by those who take their place in the 'real' world of straight, rather than gay, relationships. This point is most succinctly expressed by Adelaide Comerford, who, writing in *Films in Review,* claims that when Williams is not dealing with 'sex degenerates or other psychopaths' his 'ignorance of life is boringly patent'.[22]

This notion that the work of gay artists cannot be taken seriously because it deals with facts of feeling unknown to straights does have a certain awful logic to it.[23] People insufficiently sensitive to those aspects of our situation which give to an artist's work a measure of dignity surely cannot be expected to be open to the understandings that spring from our unique encounters with self and society. Those who malign or reject the existence of a gay sensibility will all too often overlook the fact that the feelings and creative productions of artists, gay or straight, are the sum total of their experiences—education, relationships, repressions, fortunes and misfortunes—which have entered into their inner lives. To dismiss the creative efforts that spring from such influences on the ground that the artist is gay serves no useful purpose whatsoever. Certainly it is true enough that gays *do* develop a unique perception of the world, just as do all members of minority groups which have been treated, in essential respects, as marginal to society. And since sexuality can be divorced from no aspect of the inner workings of the human personality, it cannot be divorced from creativity. What one wants to know is this: given the nature of our unique situation, what special insights does the gay artist have to offer?

In defining the gay sensibility it is important to remember that gays are members of a minority group, and that minorities have always constituted some sort of threat to the majority. Thus, gays have been regarded with fear, suspicion, and, even, hatred. The knowledge of these attitudes has developed in us what I have referred to above as a unique set of perspectives and understandings about what the world is like and how best we can deal with it. It is true that gay artists may at times protect themselves from the social pressures imposed upon them by our cultural contradictions and social prejudices. Hence, it may be that fantasies of revenge are sometimes transformed into art as a way of allowing vicarious play to erotic wishes renounced in the interests of social acceptance; resentments are expressed over treatment received; appeals for sympathy are made through the demonstration of damage wrought by continued injustice and oppression; psychic wounds are recorded so that art becomes, as Williams has said of his own work, 'an escape from a world of reality in which I felt acutely uncomfortable'[24]; female masks are donned; charades enacted; false identities assumed.

But are not such forms of expression—'deceptions'—in fact everywhere the rule? In Freud's formulation of the creative impulse, the artist is originally one who turns away from reality out of a refusal to come to terms with the demand for his or her renunciation of instinctual satisfaction, and who then, in fantasy life, allows full play to erotic and ambitious wishes.[25] Creativity is thus an inevitable outcome of repressed impulses or relationships. As such it constitutes a defiance against 'unlived life'.[26] True, the insights offered by so many of the female characters in Williams's films are the product of a gay sensibility. But then the gay artist is one who is graced with a double vision—a vision which belongs to all members of oppressed groups. Those on the outside better understand the activities of the insider than vice versa. As Benjamin DeMott has pointed out in his essay, 'But He's a Homosexual . . .', the gay artist often speaks more frankly than the straight on such matters as the tedium of marriage, the horrors of family life, the lover's exploitation of personality, and the slow erosion of character in promiscuity.[27]

If we are not too rigid about drawing the line between thought and fantasy, but, rather, conceive of creative endeavour as encompassing a great range of covert mental processes, then it should be possible to view more sympathetically Williams's female creations as important both to the conservation and change of this artist's own sense of identity, as well as for what they reveal of an aspect of love that is neither gay nor straight, but, simply, human. These are facts of feeling which gays, who have early in life recognised irony in the incompatible demands of gayness and society, cannot easily avoid. Yet these are facts which can scarcely be understood by those oblivious to the peculiarities, past or present, of our situation in the general culture.

To say this is not to suggest that *only* gays can be objective about heterosexual institutions and arrangements. It is, rather, a way of saying that gays, because of the demands constantly made upon us to justify our existence, have never been able to simply accept, passively, the cultural assumptions that non-gays may well take for granted.[28] The insights provided by, for example, the Deborah Kerr and Ava Gardner characters in *The Night of the Iguana,* are not those of 'drag queens', as has been suggested. Rather, they spring from a gay sensibility that is not so completely identified with its 'masculine' persona roles that it cannot give expression to its 'feminine' component. It is also one which refuses to lapse into unthinking acceptance of what others have insisted is appropriate behaviour for two people in love. When the Deborah Kerr character (Hannah Jelkes) speaks of her acceptance of the 'imperman-ence' of relationships, Shannon (Richard Burton) chides her, offering up the metaphor of birds who build their nests 'on the very highest level'. To this Hannah quickly replies: 'I'm not a bird, Mr. Shannon, I'm a human being. And when a member of that fantastic species builds a nest in the heart of another, the question of permanence isn't the first or even the last thing that's considered.' Echoing these sentiments precisely, the Ava Gardner character (Maxine Faulk) tells Burton that sooner or later we all reach a point where it is important to 'settle for something that works for us in our lives—even if it isn't on the highest kind of level'. This is the message advocated time and again by the Williams female, and it is very much an insight of the gay sensibility.

Conclusion

Camp and the gay sensibility have rarely, if ever, been explored in relation to cinema.[29] On the rare occasions when it has (outside of gay periodicals) analyses have tended to draw upon stereotypes of gayness with which we are all, by now, familiar. The term *camp* has been widely misused to signify the trivial, superficial and 'queer'. The original meaning and complex associations of the term, some of which I have attempted to outline in this essay, are ignored. Thus, just as it has always been a sign of worthiness to speak out on behalf of any oppressed minority group *other* than gays, so, it seems, there exists a corresponding reluctance on the part of people who take the cinema seriously (either out of contempt, or of seeming suspect, or whatever) to perceive in camp a means of heightening their appreciation of any particular performance, film or director.

Camp, as a product of the gay sensibility, has existed, right up to the present moment in time, on the same socio-cultural level as the sub-culture from which it has issued. In other words, camp, its sources and associations, have remained secret in their most fundamental aspects, just as the actual life of gays in our culture has remained secret to the overwhelming majority of non-gays. Many critics have, of course, appropriated the term *camp*, but without any understanding of its significance within the gay community. The sub-cultural attitudes, catalysts and needs that have gone to produce camp as a creative expression of gay feelings, are never considered. Yet camp is, in its essence, the expression of these feelings.

The real trouble with the usual speculations on what the critics have thought to term *camp* (aside from the fact that most of it is not) is that they never illuminate the gay sensibility, but, rather, go far to reinforce those very standards of judgment and aesthetic excellence which are often antithetical to it. It is thus that critics conclude, by implication, that camp has emerged from out of no intelligent body of socio-cultural analysis.

To say this is not, however, to plead for the application of any narrow sociological analysis. Rather, it is a way of saying that the worth of camp can simply not be understood in critical terms unless some attention is first given to the attitudes that go to produce it—attitudes which spring from our social situation and which are crucial to the development of a gay sensibility.

Notes

1. Oscar Wilde, *The Decay of Lying,* James R. Osgood, McIlvane & Co., London, 1891.
2. Susan Sontag, *Against Interpretation, and Other Essays,* Delta, New York, 1967. This point, and a number of other insights provided by Sontag in her seminal essay, 'Notes on Camp', have been most helpful to me in formulating my own ideas on the subject.
3. This point is developed by R. V. Johnson in *Aestheticism,* Methuen, London, 1969.
4. Ibid.
5. Esther Newton has explored the relationship of costume to female impersonators in *The 'Drag Queens': A Study in Urban Anthropology.* Unpublished PhD thesis, University of Chicago, 1968. I am much indebted to Newton for her insights on the style and humour systems of 'Drag Queens'.
6. W. H. Auden in his 'Introduction' to the *Intimate Journals* of Charles Pierre Baudelaire, translated by Christopher Isherwood, Methuen, London, 1949.
7. I have developed these ideas at greater length in 'Passing for Straight: The Politics of the Closet' in *Gay News* No. 62 January 1974.
8. David Thomson, *A Biographical Dictionary of the Cinema,* Secker & Warburg, London, 1975.
9. Erving Goffmann discusses the 'passing' strategy in relation to stigmatised groups in *Stigma: The Management of Spoiled Identity,* Englewood Cliffs, 1963.
10. A. R. Thompson, *The Dry Mock, A Study of Irony in Drama,* Berkeley, 1948.
11. Erving Goffman, *Stigma . . . ,* op. cit.
12. Christopher Isherwood, *The World in the Evening,* Methuen, London, 1954.
13. Thomas Elsaesser, 'A Cinema of Vicious Circles' in *Fassbinder,* Tony Rayns (ed.), BFI, London, 1976.
14. See, for example, Robin Wood, *Personal Views: Exploration in Film,* Gordon Fraser, London, 1976; and Andrew Sarris in *The Films of Josef von Sternberg,* The Museum of Modern Art/Doubleday, New York, 1966, and 'Summer Camp' in *The Village Voice,* 21.7.75.
15. Wood, *Personal Views,* op. cit.
16. Quoted in Herman Weinberg, *Josef von Sternberg, A Critical Study,* E. P. Dutton, London, 1967.
17. Ibid.
18. Claire Johnston, 'Women's Cinema as Counter-Cinema' in *Notes on Women's Cinema,* SEFT, London, 1973.
19. The *Memoirs* of Tennessee Williams, W. H. Allen, London, 1976, have also been useful to me here for the light they throw on the ways in which the author's gayness has affected his creative output.

20. The instances of critics labelling a Williams heroine 'drag queen' are too numerous to cite. However, the most extended development of this particular line of interpretation can be found in Molly Haskell, *From Reverence to Rape: The Treatment of Women in the Movies*, Penguin, New York, 1974, and Elaine Rothschild in *Films in Review*, August/September 1964, where the reviewer speaks of Williams's 'mal-formed females' and 'anti-female imagination'; see also Marjorie Rosen, *Popcorn Venus: Women, Movies and the American Dream*, Avon, New York, 1974; Foster Hirsch, 'Tennessee Williams', in *Cinema* (USA), Vol. 8, No. 1, Issue 33, Spring 1973; *The Guardian*, 27.10.76; *Interview*, April 1973.

21. Haskell, *From Reverence to Rape* . . ., op. cit.

22. *Films in Review*, December 1962.

23. Peter J. Dyer refers to the 'difficulty' of taking the film *Summer and Smoke* 'at all seriously', other than as 'a case-book study in arrested development' (in *Monthly Film Bulletin*, Vol. 29, No. 339); similarly, Molly Haskell in *From Reverence to Rape* . . . writes: 'Williams's women can be amusing company if we aren't asked to take them too seriously . . .', p. 251.

24. Tennessee Williams in *The New York Times*, 8.3.59.

25. Sigmund Freud, 'The Relation of the Poet to Daydreaming', *Collected Papers* . . ., Vol. IV, Basic Books, New York, 1959.

26. See, in this regard, Antonia Wenkart, 'Creativity and Freedom', *American Journal of Psychoanalysis*, XXIII.2 (1963).

27. Benjamin DeMott, *Supergrow: Essays and Reports on Imagination in America*, E. P. Dutton, London, 1970.

28. This so-called 'communion of touch' in relationships is further developed in the writer's *We Speak for Ourselves*, SPCK, London, 1976.

29. The notable exception is *Gay News*, a fortnightly newspaper published in London.

Notes on Recent Gay Film Criticism

by Andy Medhurst

Preliminary Remarks:

My understanding of the term 'gay film criticism' is that it denotes a politically committed intervention made by gay people into one area of the institution of cinema, namely the discursive practice of critical investigation and analysis. Its fundamental premise is a recognition of the inescapably ideological nature of both 'culture' and 'sexuality', and as a practice it seeks to explore the intersection of those two discourses, especially the intersection of the notions 'cinema' and 'homosexuality'. Its fundamental aim is (and I use these words not in any pejorative sense) utilitarian and prescriptive, setting itself the ambitious task of helping to effect social change through an engagement with filmic texts.

It is further informed by the belief that being homosexual in this culture confers particular insights into the wider mechanisms of the regulation of sexuality, and that these insights, shaped and refined by the experience of social marginalisation, instigate the keen desire for the overthrow of that regulation. The homosexual perception, precisely because of its marginalised nature, may see the order of things more clearly than those perceptions implicated in the maintenance of that order; in the words of Robin Wood:

> "In a culture in which everyone is ideologically oppressed, it is an advantage to be palbably oppressed. It is more difficult (though not of course impossible) for the heterosexual male to feel the aim of transforming ideology as a matter of urgent necessity."[1]

Whose History? -Vito Russo's "The Celluloid Closet."

Vito Russo's historical survey of representations of homosexuality in film was a book that we had needed for a very long time.[2] Prior to its long overdue publication in 1981, the only volume covering a similar field was Parker Tyler's Screening the Sexes, which was always far too eager to sacrifice analysis for artifice, ending up as little more than a series of meandering fragments held together only by its author's tiresome penchant for the linguistically baroque. It also adhered to a rigid, some might say reactionary, aesthetic hierarchy, in which various strands of avant-garde film practice were celebrated alongside certain jewels from the crown of European art cinema, leaving the mainstream American film a very poor third. Russo, thankfully, stresses the political dimension of texts, and he also prefers Hollywood. The Celluloid Closet is never less than fascinating -witty where appropriate, angry when necessary, accessible always. It is, however, deeply flawed at the conceptual level. These flaws, and they are to be found across many studies of homosexuality and culture, cohere around the problematic notion of 'gay history'. Writing in the context of feminist film theory, Claire Johnston has stated that:

"...the need for oppressed peoples to write their own histories cannot be over-stressed. Memory, an understanding of the struggles of the past and a sense of one's own history constitute a vital dynamic in any struggle."[3]

In this sense, Russo's book is invaluable. The writing of history is based on selection, which means exclusion, and exclusion is often determined by ideological concerns. Oppositional histories are needed, then, to redress the balance and correct the bias, to assert the existence and validity of those individuals, groups and events kept out of mainstream dominant history. As Russo so rightly says, "the big lie about lesbians and gay men is that we do not exist,"[4] and his book undoubtedly refutes that lie. It restores visibility, it rediscovers forgotten, neglected and suppressed moments of film history and re-examines them in the light of modern gay politics. It is, on one level, an impressive act of gay archeology.

Russo has been particularly diligent in unearthing older films (though his research is not exhaustive -he omits Chaplin's Behind the Screen, made in 1916, which contains an extended joke based on supposed homosexuality), and the most impressive section of The Celluloid Closet is its account of the 'sissy' characters that populate large numbers of musicals and comedies in the 1930s. These characters, Russo argues, represented an "outlet for unspeakable ideas."[5] In terms of other images of the period the sissies constituted a slight but real alternative to the constricting repertoire of traditional gender roles, offering the modern reader a welcome break from the negative images of later films. These films are more familiar, and about them Russo can find little new to say. He employs a predictable and reductive set of righteous dismissals, and while the political motives behind this reaction are impossible to fault, his awareness of the subtle and often contradictory functions of stereotyping appears minimal.

The fundamental problem is that for Russo, 'history' remains in the singular. He constructs his history as a single, seamless narrative, a linear 'story' of representations of homosexuality -and within this story homosexuality remains a fixed, given, essential quality which is unchanged by shifts in social, historical and ideological formations. This 'gay consciousness' is posited as some common outlook, shared worldview, or homogenous perspective that is shared by all people of an exclusively or primarily homosexual orientation. Thus sexual preference is elevated to a position of privilege over all other social and environmental factors in the construciton of the subject, while gender, age, race, class and economic power are relegated to subsidiary roles. The common ground of the current urban gay male subculture is not any intrinsic community of feeling but is dependant on specific material conditions at a specific historical conjuncture; it is determined by material factors operating on gay people (i.e. the growth of the 'pink economy' branch of capitalism) and by ideological factors operating amongst gay people.

The relevance of this tortuous digression to Russo's project is clear when we acknowledge the historicising ambitions of the 'gay consciousness' project. Not content with homogenising the present, it seeks to incorporate the past. This is more insidious, since we cannot disprove it as we can the notion of contemporary homogeneity simply by looking around us at the various realities of modern gayness, and so the 'gay consciousness' becomes, in its cultural historical mode, the 'gay sensibility'.[6] Under this banner, historical figures and cultural production from periods when our current notions of sexuality simply did not apply are assimilated into a Great Tradition, claimed as 'ours', inscribed into a retrospective fantasy which displays complete insensitivity to the delicate, complex, shifting interactions and contradictions of history. While Russo is not trying to impose a fictitious centuries-old tradition (since cinema has only existed at a time when the still dominant constructions of sexuality were more or less established) he does seem to want to blend all the varieties of gay experience, all the histories of homosexuality, into one unproblematic narrative.

The Celluloid Closet is nonetheless an important book. Given the ambitiousness of its scope, its failures are more easily understood -it is not that Vito Russo could not write a single history of representations of honosexuality, but that nobody could. Reviewing it on publication, I condescendingly called it "a telephone directory of token gays,"[7] but it is better described as a useful gathering of raw material from which more sophisticated and sensitive analysis can grow. To find such analysis we must move on from a book intended for a (comparatively) mass market and look at publications aimed at a more specific public, the specialised film journals.

In Search of the Gay Film -The "Cruising" and "Making Love" Debates.
Films concerned with homosexuality often seem to arrive in bunches. The late 1960s saw, in response to relaxed censorship laws and in relation to a number of social shifts in ideologies of sexuality, a sudden rash of films which seized on gayness as a new twist for melodrama -Reflections in a Golden Eye and The Sergeant would be two of the best-known. The very end of the 1970s and beginning of the 80s has witnessed another such eruption of Hollywood texts, and these in turn have generated a concerted response by gay criticism-the first time that such criticism, by now established as a constituent part of the radical critical agenda, could mobilise to such an extent. Films like Victor/Victoria, Personal Best and Partners feature strongly in these critical discussions, and comparisons are often made with two European films which achieved unexpected popular or critical acclaim, La Cage Aux Folles winning the former, Taxi Zum Klo securing the latter. It has, however, been two films in particular which have held the centre of the gay critical stage, Cruising and Making Love, and it is the range of responses to these that I want to focus on.

Or, more precisely, the lack of range, since the critical debate on these films has been strikingly characterised by agreement, not dissent. Cruising has come in for more frequent and more angry attacks from gays than any other film in living memory. Leaflets distributed in protest at the film stated quite simply that "People will die because of this film,"[8] a belief derived from Cruising's imputed glamourisation of the murder of homosexuals. The film was criticised for its simultaneously moralistic and voyeuristic depiction of the leather bar scene, and for its implication that homosexuality was some sort of contagious disease, a moral fungus threatening to engulf the modern city with its fondness for violent and debauched sex. Simon Watney, in by far the most considered and impressive article of this critical consensus, indicts Crusing for seeking to

"wilfully position homosexuality within a dense and mystifying field of associations with terror, violence, self-hatred and psychological disorder."[9]

Making Love, on the other hand, is derided for its pallid celebration of bourgeois monogamy. An article in Film Comment compared its attitude to homosexuality with the attitude to racial politics displayed in a film like Guess Who's Coming to Dinner -tokenistic, safe, liberal tolerance.[10] Mainstream Hollywood production, it is argued, can only address gayness if it can find ways of accommodating it within the dominant regime of sexual ideologies, so to find films which demonstrate a truly dynamic and radical approach to homosexuality we must look elsewhere. Candidates for this site of genuinely gay film practice include Taxi Zum Klo and the work of director John Waters (maker of Female Trouble and Polyester). This argument is reminiscent of the rather jaded aesthetic of Parker Tyler -Hollywood is a factory for the mass production of reactionary hegemony, only European or 'underground' cinema has any value.

It also, by implication, introduces another variant on the 'gay sensibility'. This particular manifestation of that myth is the 'gay film' -this Holy Grail, this Platonic Ideal, is assumed to be somewhere out there in the ether, waiting to be made once we have thrown off the shackles of negative stereotyping. Each film that incorporates representations of homosexuality is, in the majority of writing and discussion by gay people, implicitly measured against the mythical Gay Film, and, of course, is found wanting. Cruising and Making Love may well be misleading, distortive, even dangerous, but the films are rarely judged on their own merits or lack of them. While any examination of such films must keep in mind their relationship to prevalent discourses of sexuality, they must not be judged only by this extra-textual yardstick, and criticism must also pay close attention to their intrinsic textual dynamics.

The most common fault of over-eager ideological critiques of such films is their inability to recognise the importance of genre. Cruising, to make the point at the risk of banality, is violent partly because it is a thriller with overtones of the horror film; Making Love is concerned to advocate cosy monogamy with the Right Person because to do otherwise would wreck the project of the romantic melodrama. This is not said to excuse the clearly reactionary elements in both films, but to reassert that films 'about' homosexuality are at the same time films 'about' the codes and determinants of popular cinema. The refusal of genre comes to a head with the critical reaction to comedy. Solemnly ideological critics attack La Cage Aux Folles as politically indefensible, but prefer to ignore the much more ambiguous relationship between comedy (more of a mode than a strict genre) and ideology.[11]

I have overstated the rigidity of the consensus surrounding these films, although one does certainly exist. The best demonstration of the productive diversity of gay criticism in this area is the debate between nine male gay critics published in American Film.[12] This is stimulating primarily because of its lack of any unified position, and in the interactions between the various cultural and political stances taken by the contributors. It ranges from varieties of aestheticism and auteurism to critiques informed by sociology and psychoanalysis, includes gay-liberationist politics and politics more allied to radical Marxism, but should not be seen as a dissipation of energies. Its lack of a rigid 'party line' is exactly what makes it so refreshing, it is film criticism rather than film theory, this latter too often solidifying into an inflexible monolith which can only designate 'right' and 'wrong' positions.

Lesbian Film Criticism.

The word 'gay' sounds deceptively neutral, misleadingly inclusive, and as I demonstrated earlier is peculiarly susceptible to essentialist interpretations. And, of course, the principle specificity glossed over in essentialist constructions of gayness is that of gender. I have been guilty of that kind of glossing throughout this essay; when I have written 'gay' I should have written 'gay male', for even if there are shared concerns between lesbians and gay men (as I would hope there are) I could not claim to have the right or competence to indicate where these might lie. Thus I have been assimilating lesbian experience into what are inevitably male-defined generalisations. It is true, however, that the amount of published lesbian criticism remains tiny, so that it is not really possible to outline any definitive tendencies or particular directions within it.

Furthermore, there is an overlap between lesbian issues and the concerns of feminist criticism, so that much writing on film from a radical feminist standpoint has incorporated an awareness of lesbian perspectives. Lesbian criticism, then, has an established body of richly productive discourse, namely feminist criticism, from which to draw strength and influence. This places it in contrast to gay male criticism, which has no such established radical discourse with which to interact. To simplify this, it can be stated that there is no specific gay male sexual politics, and neither is there likely to be given the assimilatory tokenism which is happy to tolerate certain modes of gay male lifestyles while not offering such dubious crumbs to placate lesbian experience.

The March 1981 double issue of Jump Cut magazine contains an extensive special section on lesbians and film. The introduction to this special section is the nearest thing yet published to a declaration of intent for the practice of lesbian film criticism, and one of the most important points it makes is its awareness of the ambivalent nature of the relationship between lesbian concerns and feminist theory that I mentioned earlier. Feminist film theory, the authors argue, may still be constructed through heterosexual paradigms, whereas

> "A true recognition of lesbianism would seriously challenge the concept of women as inevitable objects of exchange between men...Feminist theory that sees all women on the screen only as objects of male desire (including, by implication, lesbians) is inadequate. This theoretical framework excludes lesbian experience, and it may in fact diminish the experience of all women."[13]

It is necessary, then, to assert the crucial importance of lesbianism in women's experience, and feminist film theory which continues to reproduce the primacy of heterosexuality can scarcely be called feminist at all. To prevent lesbian specificity disappearing beneath the generalised operations of feminist practice, a distinctly lesbian film criticism must be forged and utilised.

Concluding Remarks

Firstly, I am more than aware of all the vital and important work that I have omitted from this bibliographical sketch. My schematic tendencies left me no space to discuss, for example, Richard Dyer's ground-breaking studies of the relationships between codes of iconography and constructions of sexuality,[14] or Andrew Britton's eclectic investigations of figures as different as Eisenstein and Cary Grant.[15] I have also been less than fair to the high standards of film criticism in gay journals, such as that written by Jack Babuscio in the late Gay News, and that produced by a variety of writers in what are in my opinion the most consistently successful gay publications, Canada's Body Politic and Australia's Gay Information. My inadequacies with languages other than English and schoolboy French have also barred me from appreciating much material, and the limitations of my gender inevitably restrict my ability from fully comprehending other crucial fields.

I don't want to indulge in any pointless speculation as to the future directions of gay film criticism, since I believe it to be a practice which is structured by historical and ideological factors, and I would not dare to predict possible shifts in those. Instead of a neat conclusion, then, I offer a few, self-consciously pompous sentences.

Gay film criticism is not a discrete discourse, it does not even have its own unique methodology. It forms part of a wider repertoire of radical film criticisms, which at this historical moment are still finding the methodologies formed in the context of post-1968 France to be the most productive, and these are in turn part of a general cultural activism. Gay film criticism shares with its sibling radicalisms the recognition of cinema as a complex of institutions and practices positioned within historically specific social and ideological formations. It rejects, as must all radical approaches to film, any notions of 'objectivity', which it identifies as a hegemonic pretence. It must be constantly aware of all relevant developments in allied fields such as sexual politics and film theory, and it must then consider these in terms of its own specific problematic (the cluster of discourses around the notion 'homosexuality'). To do otherwise, to concern itself only with addressing its own private issues, is to run the grave risk of gay film criticism ending up in a lavender vacuum.

Notes

1. Robin Wood, review of books by Richard Dyer, Film Comment, Jan-Feb 1980, p. 71.
2. My comments on The Celluloid Closet are very strongly indebted to Richard Dyer's review of the book that appeared in Gay Information, 9/10, Autumn/Winter 1982. I have also reworked some formulations from my own original review of the book, in Framework 18, 1982.
3. Claire Johnston, The Work of Dorothy Arzner, London, British Film Institute, 1975, p. 2.

4. Vito Russo, The Celluloid Closet, New York, Harper and Row, 1981, p. xii.

5. Ibid, p. 32.

6. Jack Babuscio's essay in the present volume is by far the most impressive account of the 'gay sensibility,' and I would not want to label it with most of my criticisms of less thoughtful approaches.

7. In Framework 18, p. 54.

8. Quoted in Russo, p. 238.

9. Simon Watney, "Hollywood's Homosexual World," Screen, Vol. 23, No. 3/4, 1982, p. 120.

10. Mary Richards, "The Gay Deception," Film Comment, May-June 1982. It is worth noting that Richards is emphatically identified as nor being gay, which might make her informed heterosexual concern for the misrepresentation of gays interestingly similar to the liberal tokenism she is so quick to condemn.

11. See Carolyn Durham, "The Inversion of Laughter," Jump Cut, 27, 1982, and Ed Sikov, "Homosexuals, Bandits and Gangsters," Cineaste, Vol. 11, No. 4, 1982 for the anti-comedy lobby. For some interesting exxploratory work looking at television comedy and ideology, see Jim Cook ed, Television Sitcom, London, British Film Institute, 1982.

12. Al LaValley, "Out of the Closet and on to the Screen," American Film, Sept. 1982.

13. Edith Becker, Michele Citron, Julia Lesage and B. Ruby Rich, "Introduction to 'Lesbians and Film'," Jump Cut, 24/25, March 1981.

14. See Richard Dyer, "Don't Look Now-The Male Pin-up," Screen, Vol. 23, No. 3-4, 1982; "Seen to be Believed," Studies in Visual Communication, Vol. 9, 9, No. 2, Spring 1983.

15. See Andrew Britton, "Sexuality and Power," Framework 6; Cary Grant: Comedy and Male Desire, Newcastle, Tyneside Cinema, 1983.

Susanah York, Beryl Reid and Coral Browne at the Gateways Club in THE KILLING OF SISTER GEORGE.

Chris Sarandon as the suicidal Leon in DOG DAY AFTERNOON.

Mariel Hemingway and Patrice Donnelly star in PERSONAL BEST as two Olympic track contenders who become lovers and eventual competitors.

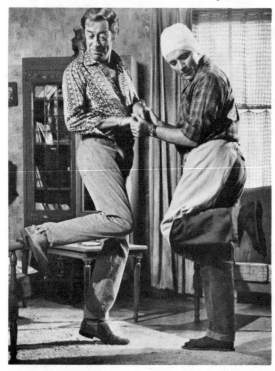

Charlie (Rex Harrison) and Harry (Richard Burton) celebrate Charlie's commercial in Stanley Donen's STAIRCASE.

Peter Finch and Murray Head in John Schlesinger's SUNDAY BLOODY SUNDAY.

Michael Ontkean, Kate Jackson and Harry Hamlin in MAKING LOVE as three young people who must reassess the meaning of love.

The patrons of The Blue Joy Bar try to raise the spirits of a lovesick waiter (Nick De Noia) in SOME OF MY BEST FRIENDS ARE. . . .

Kenneth Nelson, Cliff Gorman, and Robert La Tourneaux in William Friedkin's BOYS IN THE BAND.

Filmography

This is a listing of films which contain representations of gay women and men. It does not include films which might be termed gay even though there are no gay characters as such in them. It excludes films made for television.

Although the aim of the list is to be inclusive rather than exclusive, there have been many problems in compiling it. Firstly, titles are constantly coming to light and new films are being released. In this sense, the filmography is still in progress rather than definitely completed. Second, our ignorance in the West of the cinemas of Asia, Africa and South America still means that there is probably an enormous number of titles from these areas missing. (I cannot believe, for instance, that the three titles I have for Japan actually constitute its output in this area.) Third, the area of pornography is very hard to keep track of, especially if one wanted to take into account (as I have not) 8mm productions. Fourth, and most problematic, it is not always easy to determine whether a character in a film is gay or not. In early examples it is all done by inference and suggestion, and it is often hard to be sure whether one's interpretation of a character as gay is really warranted. Then, what do you with the 'buddy ' movies – do you include *Thunderbolt and Lightfoot,* for instance? And if that, how about the Redford-Newman films? And should one include the type of film discussed by Caroline Sheldon as being 'politically' lesbian? On the whole, I have restricted myself to cases where the film itself clearly intends one to understand the character as gay, although I have been inclined to give myself more leeway in relation to earlier films since they are so much rarer. This last point relates to the fifth problem I had in compiling the list, namely, the fact that so often gay characters are only on screen for a few seconds, especially for a passing joke or to give the film a frisson of decadence. Once one starts including all these appearances the list becomes massive – especially as in recent years a gay spot like this seems to have become almost obligatory as the token black character. In selecting here, I have tended to include only those cases which either occupy a substantial amount of screen time or are integrated into the plot of the film.

One or two interesting points emerge from this listing. Given the extent to which they have been excluded from the position, women figure heavily as directors, and not only in films depicting lesbianism (*e.g.* Audry, Beeson, Chytilova, Clarke, Hammer, Kaplan, Oxenburg, Rothman, Sagan, Zetterling etc.). The four earliest examples – *Anders als die Anderen, Die Büchse von Pandora, Mikael, Mädchen in Uniform* – are all German. As one has, regretfully, to expect, 'communist' countries are conspicuous by their absence, although there are examples from Czechoslovakia and Yugoslavia. Again as expected, pornographic titles figure heavily, and there is an enormous increase in titles after the mid-sixties.

The listing is alphabetical by title. After the title the following information is given – country of production; date; director (surname in brackets); principal performers (including where possible the name of the performers of gay parts); a reference from which further information can be obtained. Where possible, I have for the latter used *The Monthly Film Bulletin (MFB).* The abbreviations for other references are listed at the end.   R.D.

Abduction; USA, 1975; (Zito); Judith-Marie Bergan, David Pendleton; *MFB* 43, p. 143.
Adam and Yves; USA; (de Rome).
Advise and Consent; USA, 1961–2; (Preminger); Don Murray; *MFB* 29, p. 122.

Akujo (Night Scandal in Japan); Jap, 1964; (Watanabe); Mayumi Ogawa, Muko Midoui; *MFB* 35, p. 57.
A lira do delirio; Braz, 1977; (Lima); Anecy Rocha, Cláudio Marco; *Filme Cultura* no. 29, p. 65–6.
All about Alice; S, p. 191.
Alpenglühn im Dirndlrock (Stop It – I like it); Ger, 1974; (Götz); Elisabeth Volkmann, Rinaldo Talamonti; *MFB* 43, p. 211.
Älskande Par (Loving Couples); Swed, 1965; (Zetterling); Harriet Andersson, Gio Petré; *MFB* 32, p. 130.
Alta infedelta; Fr/It, 1963; (Rossi); John Philip Law, Nino Manfredi; *Variety* 26.2.64, p. 6.
Altra faccia del peccato, l' (The Queer . . . the Erotic); It, 1969; (Avallone); *MFB* 37, p. 61.
Alyse et Chloë; Fr, 1970; (Gainville); Katrin Jacobsen, Michèle Girardon; *MFB* 38, p. 43.
amitiés particulières, Les; Fr, 1964; (Delannoy); Didier Haudepin, Michel Bouquet; *film français* 11.9.64, p. 10.
American Cream; USA, 1972; *Mandate* Feb 72.
Amerikanische Soldat, Der; Ger, 1970; (Fassbinder); Karl Scheydt, Ulli Lommel; *MFB* 45, p. 111.
Amor bandido; Braz, 1978; (Barreto); Paulo Gracindo, Cristina Achê; *Filme Cultura* no. 31, p. 95–7.
amour comme le nôtre, Un (French Love); Fr/It/Can, 1974; (Marchand); Paola Senatore, Mauro Parenti; *MFB* 42, p. 195.
amour humain, L'; Can, 1970; (Héroux); Jacques Riberolles, Louise Marleau; *MFB* 39, p. 91.
Amphetamine; USA, 1966; (Sonbert & Appel).
Ander, De; Neths, 1966; (Terpstra); Scheugl, p. 281.
Anders als die Anderen; Ger, 1919; (Oswald); Conrad Veidt, Reinhold Schünzel; Scheugl, pp. 157–8.
Anders als Du und Ich (Das Dritte Geschlecht; The Third Sex); Ger. 1957; (Harlan); Christian Wolff, Paula Wessley; *MFB* 26, p. 42.
Anderson Tapes, The; USA, 1971, (Lumet); Sean Connery, Martin Balsam; *MFB* 38, p. 235.
And Now My Love (see *Toute une vie*).
Anima Nera; It, 1962 (Rossellini); Eleonora Rossi-Drago, Vittorio Gassman; Guarner, pp. 100–3.
Anita; Swed, 1974; (Wickman); Christine Lindberg, Stella Skarsgard; *MFB* 42, p. 235.
Ann and Eve (Anybody's); Swed, 1969; (Mattsson); Gio Petré, Marie Liliedahl; *MFB* 37, p. 183.
Anna und Elizabeth; Ger, 1933; (Wysbar); Dorothea Wieck, Hertha Thiele; Eisner, p. 326, 348.
Anomalies; S, p. 93.
Ansikte mot Ansikte (Face to Face); Swed, 1975; (Bergman); Liv Ullmann, Erland Josephson; *MFB* 43, p. 247.
Anybody's (see *Ann and Eve*).
Any Time Anywhere (see *Les liaisons particulières*).
Arabian Nights (see *Il fiore delle mille e una notte*).
Are You Being Served?; GB, 1977; (Kellett); John Inman; *MFB* 44, p. 188.
Armee der Liebenden oder Aufstand der Perversen; Ger, 1979; (von Praunheim); *Variety* 21.3.79, p. 28.
Arturo's Island (see *L'isola di Arturo*).
Ash Wednesday; USA, 1973; (Peerce); Elizabeth Taylor, Keith Baxter; *MFB* 41, p. 68.
Assassino . . . é al telefono (The Killer is on the Phone); It, 1972 (de Martino); Telly Savalas, Rossella Falk; *MFB* 42, p. 256.
August and July; Can, 1973; (Markowitz); Sharon Smith, Alexa Dewiel; *Variety* 11.4.73, p. 61.
A un dios desconocido (To an unknown God); Sp, 1977; (Chavarri); Hector Alterio, Javier Elorriaga; *Variety* 28.9.77, p. 24.
Au royaume des cieux (Women Hunt); Fr, 1949; (Duvivier); Suzanne Cloutier, Serge Reggiani; *MFB* 18, p. 227.
Aus eines Marines Mädchenjahren; Ger, 1919; (Grunne); Scheugl, p. 158.

Baby Love; GB, 1968; (Reid); Linda Hayden, Diana Dors; *MFB* 36, p. 79.

Back Row, The; USA, 1973; (Richards); Cal Culver; *Variety* 21.2.73, p. 24.

Bara No Soretsu (Funeral Parade of Roses); Jap, 1970; (Matsumoto); Peter, Osamu Ogasawara; *Variety* 8.11.70, p. 40.

Barbarella; Fr, 1967; (Vadim); Jane Fonda, Anita Pallenberg; *MFB* 35, p. 167.

Bavarian Hunting Scenes (see *Jagdszenen aus Niederbayern*).

beau mec, Le; Fr, 1978; (Potts); Karl Forest, Cedric Dumont; *Cinéma 79*, no. 247–8, pp. 133–4.

Bed, The; USA, 1967; (Broughton); Gary Graham, p. 52.

Behind the Green Door; USA; (Mitchell Brothers); Marilyn Chambers; *S,* p. 177.

Best Way to Get Along, The (see *La meilleure façon de marcher*).

Betsy, The; USA, 1978 (Petrie); Paul Rudd, Clifford David; *MFB* 45, pp. 84–5.

Beverley Hills Call Boys, The; USA, 1970; (Desimore); Scott Arden, Joey Latti; *Variety* 11.11.70, p. 22.

Beyond Good and Evil (see *Oltre il bene e il male*).

Beyond the Valley of the Dolls; USA, 1970; (Meyer); Dolly Read, Cynthia Myers; *MFB* 38, p. 45.

biches, Les; Fr/It, 1967; (Chabrol); Stéphane Audran, Jacqueline Sassard; *MFB* 36, p. 23.

Bigger Splash, A; GB, 1974; (Hazan); David Hockney, Peter Schlesinger; *MFB* 42, p. 76.

Big Snatch, The; USA, (Friedman); *S,* p. 43.

Bijou; USA, 1972; (Poole); Bill Harrison, Tom Bradford; *Variety* 18.10 72, p. 18.

bijoux de famille, Les (French Blue); Fr, 1974; (Laureux); Françoise Brion, Corinne O'Brian; *MFB* 43, p. 144.

Bike Boy; USA, 1967; (Warhol); Joe Spencer, Ed Hood; *MFB* 37, pp. 243–4.

Bildnis des Dorian Gray, Das; Ger/It/Liechtenstein, 1970; (Dallamano); Helmut Berger, Richard Todd, Herbert Lom; *MFB* 40, pp. 144–5.

Bilitis; Fr, 1976; (Hamilton); Patricia d'Arbanville, Mona Kristensen; *MFB* 45, p. 112.

Bitteren Tränen der Petra von Kant, Die; Ger, 1972; (Fassbinder); Irm Hermann, Margit Carstensen; *MFB* 42, p. 99.

Bizarre Sex Practices; S, p. 93.

Black Emmanuelle (see *Emmanuelle Nera*).

Black Flowers for the Bride (Something for Everyone); USA, 1970; (Prince); Michael York, Anthony Corlan; *MFB* 38, p. 137.

Black Heat, Sexuality in The Movies, p. 162.

Black Leather Pants (see *Geh, Zieh dein Dirndl aus*).

Blackstar: Autobiography of a Friend; USA 1977; (Joslin); *Jump Cut* no. 20, p. 9.

Blacula; USA, 1972; (Crain); William Marshall, Denise Nicholas; *MFB* 40, pp. 188–9.

Bloedverwanten (Blood Relations); Neths/Fr, 1977; (Lindner); Maxim Hamel, Sophie Deschamps; *MFB* 46, p. 21.

Blood and Roses (see *Et mourir de plaisir*).

Blood Relations (see *Bloedverwanten*).

Blow Job; USA, 1964; (Warhol); *Film Culture* no. 37, p. 20.

Blue Belle (see *La fine dell'innocenza*).

Blue Jeans; Fr, 1977; (des Roziers); Gilles Budin, Michel Gibet; *Ecran* no. 56, p. 68.

Blue Sextet; USA, 1969; (Durston); John Damon, Peter Clune; *MFB* 39, p. 247.

Bob and Daryll and Ted and Alex; S, p. 191.

Bögjävlar (Damned Queers); Swed, 1977; (Filmgruppen).

bonzesse, La; Fr, 1974; (Jouffa); Sylvie Meyer, Bernard Varley; *MFB* 42, p. 151.

Born to Raise Hell; Mandate Feb 77.

Boy called Third Base, A (see *Sado*).

Boy Friend 2; Fr, 1977; (Soukaz); *Ecran* no. 57, p. 3.

Boys and Girls Together; GB, 1979; (Marsden); Paul Ong, Helen Fitzgerald; *MFB* 47, p. 44.

Boys and the Bandit, The; S, p. 191.

Boys in the Band, The; USA, 1970; (Friedkin); Leonard Frey, Kenneth Nelson; *MFB* 37, p. 199.

Boys in the Sand; USA, 1971; (Poole); Cal Culver, Peter Fisk; *Variety* 22.12.71, p. 6.

Branded for Life (see *Marcados para viver*).

71

Brute Force; USA, 1947; (Dassin); Hume Cronyn, Burt Lancaster; *MFB* 14, p. 113.
Büchse von Pandora, Die; Ger, 1928; (Pabst); Louise Brooks, Alice Roberts; *MFB* 41, p. 111.
Busting; USA, 1973; (Hyams); Elliott Gould, Robert Blake; *MFB* 41, pp. 24–5.
Butley; USA/GB/Can, 1973; (Pinter); Alan Bates, Michael Byrne; *MFB* 43, p. 25.

Cabaret; USA, 1972; (Fosse); Michael York, Helmut Griem; *MFB* 39, p. 108.
Cactus in the Snow (see *You Can't Have Everything*).
caduti degli dei, La (Götterdämmerung; The Damned); It, 1970; (Visconti); Dirk Bogarde, Ingrid Thulin; *MFB* 37, p. 95.
cage aux folles, La; Fr/It, 1978; (Molinaro); Michel Serrault, Ugo Tognazzi; *MFB* 47, p. 5.
Caged; USA, 1950; (Cromwell); Eleanor Parker, Agnes Moorehead; *MFB* 17, p. 134.
Calde labbra; It, 1976; (Dani); Caludine Beccarie, Leonora Fani; *MFB* 44, p. 208.
Can You Keep It Up for a Week?; GB, 1974; (Atkinson); Jeremy Bulloch, Jill Damas; *MFB* 41, p. 270.
carnet rose d'un homosexuel, Le; Fr, 1971; (Smalto/Tense); Benoit Archenoul, Claude Loir; *Ecran* no. 62, p. 65.
Carry On series; GB, 1958–.
Casey; Cal Culver; *S,* p. 206.
Cat on a Hot Tin Roof; USA, 1958; (Brooks); Paul Newman, Elizabeth Taylor; *MFB* 25, p. 139.
Ceremonia sangrieta (Ritual of Blood); Sp/It, 1972; (Grau); Ewa Aulin, Lucia Bose; *Vampire,* pp. 102–3.
chant d'amour, Un; Fr, 1950; (Genet); *MFB* 40, p. 236.
Charlotte (La jeune fille assassinée); Fr/It/Ger, 1974; (Vadim); Sirpa Lane, Roger Vadim; *MFB* 44, p. 44.
Charlys Nichten (Confessions of a Sexy Photographer); Ger, 1974; (Boos); Josef Moosholzer, Bertram Edelmann; *MFB* 43, p. 164.
chatte sans pudeur, La (Sexy Lovers); Fr, 1974; (Angel); Danie Danyel, Nadine Perks; *MFB* 42, p. 152.
Chelsea Girls, The; USA, 1967; (Warhol); Robert Olivier, Mary Woronow; *MFB* 39, pp. 134–5.
Children; GB, 1974; (Davies); *BNFC* vol. 16, 1978.
Children's Hour, The (see *The Loudest Whisper*).
Christine Jorgensen Story, The; USA, 1970; (Rapper); John Hansen; *MFB* 37, p. 224.
Chumlum; USA, 1964; (Rice); Jack Smith, Mario Montez; *Film Culture* no. 48–9, p. 30.
Cleopatra Jones; USA, 1973; (Starrett); Shelley Winters, Tamara Dobson; *MFB* 40, p. 14.
Clockwork Nympho (see *Les mille et une perversions de Felicia*).
Close Encounters of a Handyman (see *Ein guter Hahn wird selten fett*).
Collection, The; S, p. 189.
collégiennes, Les (The Twilight Girls); Fr, 1956; (Hunebelle); Gaby Morlay, Henri Guisol; *MFB* 29, p. 39.
Comedy in Six Unnatural Acts; USA, 1975; (Oxenburg); *BNFC* vol. 16, 1978.
Come One, Come All; (Friedman); *S,* p. 43.
Come Together; GB, 1971; (Shane); *MFB* 39, p. 39.
Coming Out; USA, 1973; (Berkeley Lesbian Feminist Film Collective); Dawson, p. 12.
comtesse aux seins nus, La; Belg, 1975; (Johnson (Franco)); Lina Ronay, Alica Arno; *MFB* 45, p. 217.
Confessions of a series; GB, 1973–.
Confessions of a Male Groupie; USA, 1971; (de Simone & Grippo); Scheugl, p. 280.
Confessions of a Sexy Photographer (see *Charlys Nichten*).
confidences de Sandra, Les; Fr, 1973; (Aubin); Manuelle Olivier, Dany William; *MFB* 42, p. 77.
Conformist, The; It/Fr/Ger, 1969; (Bertolucci); Jean-Louis Trintignant, Dominique Sanda; *MFB* 38, p. 237.
Congés payés 36; (Beauvais).
Contes immoraux; Fr, 1974; (Borowczyk); Paloma Picasso, Pascale Christophe; *MFB* 44, pp. 120–1.

Continuing Story of Carel and Fred, The; USA, 1972; (Ginsberg); Vogel, p. 221.
Continuous Woman, The; (Twin Cities Film Collective); *Women and Film* 5/6, p. 81.
Conversation Piece (see *Gruppo di famiglia in un interno*).
Coonskin; USA, 1975; (Bakshi); Barry White, Charles Gordone; *Variety* 13.8.75, p. 16.
corps de Diane, Le; Fr, 1969; (Richard); Jeanne Moreau.
Couch; USA, 1964; (Warhol); Gerard Malanga, Naomi Levine, Jack Kerouac, Allen Ginsberg.
Couronne d'or; Fr; (Velon); de Becker, p. 134.
Craving for Lust, A; Gr, 1975?; (Mastorakis); Bob Belling, Jane Ryall; *MFB* 45, p. 5.
Cross of Iron; GB/Ger, 1977; (Peckinpah); James Coburn, Roger Fritz; *MFB* 44, pp. 40–1.
Cruising; USA, 1980; (Friedkin); Al Pacino, Richard Cox; *Variety* 13.2.80, p. 16.
Cumulus Nimbus; USA; (Giritlian); Dawson, p. 39.
Curse of the Flesh, The; USA; (Riva & Marsh); S, pp. 23–4.

Daddy Darling; USA, 1970; (Sarno); Helle Louise, Gio Petré; *MFB* 39, p. 110.
Damned, The (see *La Caduti degli Dei*).
Dance of the Vampires; GB, 1967; (Polanski); Roman Polanski, Ferdy Mayne; *MFB* 36, p. 4.
Dany la ravageuse; Fr, 1972; (Rozier); Sandra Jullien; *MFB* 39, p. 185.
Darling; GB, 1965; (Schlesinger); Julie Christie, Dirk Bogarde; *MFB* 32, p. 132.
Daughters of Anomaly; S, p. 93.
Daughters of Darkness (see *La rouge aux lèvres*).
Daughters of Lesbos, The; S, p. 24.
David is Homosexual; GB, 1978; (Avery/Lewisham CHE); Ray McLaughlin.
Day of the Jackal, The; GB/Fr, 1973; (Zinnemann); Edward Fox; *MFB* 40, pp. 122–3.
Deadfall; GB, 1968; (Forbes); Michael Caine, Eric Portman; *MFB* 35, p. 178.
Dead Youth; USA, 1967; (Richie).
Dead of Summer (see *Ondate di calore*).
Death in Venice (see *Morte a Venezia*).
Death of Maria Malibrau (see *Der Tod der Maria Malibrau*).
Deep Compassion, A; USA, 1972; (Kingston); *Sexuality in the Movies*, p. 162.
Deliverance; USA, 1972; (Boorman); Jon Voigt, Burt Reynolds; *MFB* 39, pp. 186–7.
Desirella (The Sextrovert); Fr, 1970; (Dague); Jean-Claude Bouillon, Sabine Sun; *MFB* 38, p. 95.
désir et la volupté, Le (Lust and Desire); Fr, 1973; (Saint-Clair); Claire Gregory, Denise Roland; *MFB* 42, p. 102.
Desperate Living; USA, 1977; (Waters); Susan Lowe, Liz Renay; *MFB* 34, pp. 132–3.
Detective, The; USA, 1968; (Douglas); Frank Sinatra, Tony Musante; *MFB* 35, p. 148.
Deutschland im Herbst; Ger, 1978; (Fassbinder *(et al.)*); Rainer Werner Fassbinder, Armin Meier; *MFB* 46, pp. 5–6.
Devil in Miss Jones, The; USA, 1973; (Damiano); Georgina Spelvin; S, p. 184.
Devil in the Flesh; (Hall); Mark Taylor, Brian Reynolds; S, p. 195.
Devil Queen (see *Arainha diaba*).
Diamonds Are Forever; GB, 1971; (Hamilton); Sean Connery; *MFB* 39, pp. 29–30.
Diario segreto da un carcere femminile (Love in a Women's Prison); It, 1972; (Silvestro); Anita Strindbeg, Eva Czemerys; *MFB* 42, p. 236.
Diary of a Mad Housewife; USA, 1970; (Perry); Frank Langella, Carrie Snodgrass; *MFB* 38, p. 162.
Differente; Sp, 1961; (Delgado); Alfredo Alaria, Sandro Lebroc; *MFB* 29, p. 135.
Different Story, A; USA, 1978; (Aaron); Perry King, Meg Foster; *MFB* 46, pp. 144–5.
Dinah East; USA; (Nash); Ultra Violet, Andy Davis; *Filmfacts* vol. 14 no. 24, p. 707.
diputado, El; Sp, 1978; (de la Inglesia).
Dirty Mary (see *La fiancée du pirate*).
disordine, Il (Verwirrung); It, 1962; (Brusati); Renato Salvatori, Louis Jourdan; *Variety* 16.5.62.
Django Kill (see *Gringo uccidi*).
Dr Jekyll and Sister Hyde; GB, 1971; (Baker); Ralph Bates, Martine Beswick; *MFB* 38, p. 218.

Doctors' Wives; USA, 1970; (Schaefer); Richard Crenna, Janice Rule; *MFB* 38, p. 162.
Doctor in the Nude (see *Traitement de choc*).
Dog Day Afternoon; USA, 1975; (Lumet); Al Pacino, Chris Sarandon; *MFB* 42, p. 236.
dolce vita, La; It, 1960; (Fellini); Marcello Mastroianni; *MFB* 28, p. 4.
Donnez-nous notre amour quotidien (In love with sex); It/Fr/Can, 1973; (Pierson); Paola Senatore, Lucretia Lore; *MFB* 41, p. 96.
Dorian Gray (see *Das bildnis des Dorian Gray*).
Dracula's Daughter; USA, 1936; (Hillyer); Otto Kruger, Gloria Holden; *MFB* 3, p. 115.
Drifter; (Rocco); *S*, p. 114.
Dritte Geschlecht, Das (see *Anders als du und ich*).
Drum; USA, 1976; (Carver); Warren Oates, Ken Norton; *MFB* 43, p. 212.
Duffer; GB, 1971; (des Pins & Dumaresq); Kit Gleave, Erna May; *MFB* 39, p. 30.
Dyketactics; USA; (Hammer); Dawson, p. 45.
Dzieje Grzechu (The Story of Sin); Pol, 1975; (Borowczyk); Malek Walczewski; *MFB* 43, p. 78.

Earth Child; S; p. 189.
Echoes of Silence; USA, 1965; (Goldman); Miguel Chacour, Viraj Amonsi; *F & F* vol. 15 no. 12, pp. 67–8.
Eiger Sanction, The; USA 1975; (Eastwood); Clint Eastwood, Jack Cassidy; *MFB* 42, p. 173.
El Paso Wrecking Company, The; USA, 1977; (Cage).
Emily; GB, 1976; (Herbert); Koo Stark, Ina Skriver; *MFB* 44, p. 6.
Emmanuelle; Fr, 1974; (Jaeckin); Sylvia Kristel, Marika Green; *MFB* 41, p. 223.
Emmanuelle II, l'anti-vierge; Fr, 1975; (Giacobetti); Sylvia Kristel; *MFB* 43, p. 250.
Emmanuelle Nera; It, 1976; (Thomas); *MFB* 43, p. 146.
Emperor Tomato Ketchup.
Encounter; 1971; (de Rome); Scheugl, p. 282.
Ende des Regenbogens, Das; Ger, 1979; (Friessner).
Engelchen macht weiter, hoppe hoppe Reiter; Ger, 1968; (Verhoeren); Mario Adorf, Gila von Weitershausen; Scheugl, p. 160.
Entertaining Mr. Sloane; GB, 1969; (Hickox); Beryl Reid, Harry Andrews; *MFB* 37, p. 72.
Equilibrium (The Other Sex); Nor, 1965; (Muller); Guri Heitmann Muller, Per Christensen; *MFB* 35, p. 40.
Ernesto; It/Sp/Ger, 1979; (Samperi); Martin Halm, Virna Lisi; *Variety* 7.3.79, p. 22.
Erotic Eva (see *Eva Nera*).
Erotic Fantasies; GB, 1971; (Leigh); *MFB* 39, p. 50.
Erotic Three, The; USA, 1969; (Matter); Harry Walker Staff, Victoria Wilde; *MFB* 38, p. 72.
Erotikus; (Halsted); *S*, p. 193.
érotisme à l'étude, L' (My Body Burns); Fr, 1973; (Pallardy); Evelyne Scott, Claude Sandron; *MFB* 41, p. 273.
Escape, The (see *La fuga*).
Eskimo Nell; GB, 1975; (Campbell); Michael Armstrong, Terence Edmond; *MFB* 41, pp. 273–4.
Es war nicht die Nachtigall (Julia); Ger, 1974; (Rothermund); Sylvia Kristel, Grisela Hahn; *MFB* 42, p. 174.
Et mourir de plaisir (Blood and Roses); Fr/It, 1960; (Vadim); Annette Stroyberg, Elsa Martinelli; *MFB* 29, p. 5.
Eva nera (Erotic Eva); It, 1976; (d'Amato); Laura Gemser, Jack Palance; *MFB* 44, p. 122.
Exhibition; Fr, 1975; (Davy); Claudine Beccarie; *MFB* 43, p. 213.
Experiment, The; USA, 1975; (Hall & Knight); Mike Stevens, Joey Daniels; *S*, p. 195.

Face to Face (see *Ansikte mot Ansikte*).
Falconhead; USA, 1976; (Zen); *Mandate* Feb 77.
Farewell My Lovely; USA, 1975; (Richards); Robert Mitchum, Kate Murtagh; *MFB* 42. p. 259.
Faster Pussycat! Kill! Kill!; USA, 1966; (Meyer); Tura Satana, Haji; *Variety* 9.2.66.
Fast Kill, The; USA, 1972; (Schonteff); Tom Adams, Susie Hampton; *MFB* 39, p. 231.
Faustrecht der Freiheit (Fox and his Friends); Ger, 1975; (Fassbinder); Rainer Werner Fassbinder, Peter Chatel; *MFB* 43, p. 6.

Feelings; GB, 1975; (Britten); Kate O'Mara; *MFB* 43, p. 165.

femme, un jour, Une; Fr, 1976; (Keigel); Caroline Cellier, Melanie Brevan; *Variety* 2.2.77, p. 22.

Feuerzeichen; Ger, 1979; (Bold).

fiancée du pirate, La; Fr, 1969; (Kaplan); Bernadette Lafont, Claire Maurier; *MFB* 39, p. 161.

fille aux yeux d'or, La; Fr, 1961; (Albicocco); Marie Laforet, Paul Guers; *MFB* 29, p. 75.

fine dell'innocenze, La; GB/It, 1975; (Dallamo); Annie Belle, Charles Fawcett; *MFB* 44, pp. 39–40.

fiore delle mille e una notte, Il (Arabian Nights); It/Fr, 1974; (Pasolini); Ninetto Davoli, Franco Citti; *MFB* 42, p. 79.

Fire Island; S, p. 191.

Fire Island Fever; USA, 1979; (Deveau); John Carlo, Garry Hunt; *Body Politic* Dec. 1979, p. 32.

Fire Island Kids; 1971; (de Rome); Scheugl, p. 282.

Fireworks; USA, 1947; (Anger).

First Time Around; (Brian); *S,* pp. 191, 195.

Five in Hand; (Brian); *S,* p. 189.

Flaming Creatures; USA, 1962; (Smith); *Film Culture* no. 29, p. 4.

Flesh; USA, 1968; (Morrissey); Joe Dallesandro, Geraldine Smith; *MFB* 37, pp. 45–6.

Flesh Gordon; USA, 1974; (Benveniste/Ziehn); Jason Williams; *MFB* 42, p. 55.

Flower Thief, The; USA, 1960; (Rice); Taylor Mead, Philip McKenna; *Variety* 4.6.69, p. 6.

Fortune and Men's Eyes; USA/Can, 1971; (Hart); Wendell Burton, Zooey Hall; *MFB* 39, p. 51.

Four more than Money; (Brian); Joe Markham; *S,* p. 195.

Fox and his Friends (see *Faustrecht der Freiheit*).

Fox, The; USA, 1967; (Rydell); Sandy Dennis, Anne Heywood; *MFB* 35, p. 91.

Fragment of Seeing; 1946; (Harrington); Vogel, p. 244.

Fräulein Doktor; Yug/It, 1969; (Lattuada); Suzy Kendall, Capucine; *MFB* 37, pp. 185–6.

Frau sucht Liebe, Eine; Ger, 1968; (Azderball); Eva Renzi, Barbara Rütting; *MFB* 37, p. 13.

Freiheit für die Liebe; Ger, 1969; (Kronhausen); *Variety* 17.6.70, p. 16.

French Blue (see *Les bijoux de famille*).

French Governess, The (see *Calda labbra*).

French Love (see *Un amour comme le nôtre*).

Friday on my mind; S, p. 189.

Friday 13th; GB, 1976; (Sessler); *BNFC* vol. 14.

frisson des vampires, Le; Fr, 1970; (Rollin); Sandra Julien; *MFB* 44, p. 219.

From Russia with Love; GB, 1963; (Young); Sean Connery, Lotte Lenya; *MFB* 30, p. 155.

Fuego (Passionate Desires); Arg, 1969; (Bo); Isabel Sarli, Armando Bo; *MFB* 44, p. 147.

Fuga, La (The Escape); It/Fr, 1964; (Spinola); Anouk Aimée, Giovanna Ralli; *Variety* 7.4.65.

Funeral Parade of Roses (see *Bara no soretsu*).

Funny Lady; USA, 1975; (Ross); Barbra Streisand, Roddy McDowell; *MFB* 42, pp. 106–7.

Galia; It/Fr, 1966; (Lautner); Mireille Darc, Françoise Prevost; *MFB* 33, p. 93.

Games, The; USA, 1969; (Winner); Stanley Baker, Michael Crawford; *MFB* 37, pp. 165–6.

Gangstermeisje, Het, (A gangster girl); Neths, 1967; (Weisz); Walter Kous, Joop van Hulzen; *Variety* 5.7.67, pp. 6, 24.

garces, Les (Love Hungry Girls); Fr/It, 1973; (Angel); Jackie Lombard, Marika Pica; *MFB* 40, p. 248.

garçonne, La; Fr, 1957; (Audry); Andrée Debar, Marie Deams; *MFB* 25 p. 76.

Gates to Paradise; GB/Ger, 1967; (Wajda); Lionel Stander, Ferdy Mayne; *Variety* 3.7.68, p. 28.

Gay Day, A; USA, 1973; (Hammer); Dawson, p. 45.

Gay Deceivers, The; USA, 1969; (Kessler); Kevin Coughlin, Lawrence Casey; *MFB* 37, p. 80.

Gay Guide to Hawaii; S, p. 191.

Gay Parade; USA, 1972; (Rubin).

Gay, Proud and Sober; USA; (Star Films).

Gay USA; USA; (Bressau); *Film Quarterly* vol.32 no.2, pp. 50–7.

Geh, zieh dein Dirndl aus (Black Leather Pants); Ger, 1972; (Götz); Rinaldo Talamonti, Elizabeth Volkmann; *MFB* 43, p. 147.
Gelbe Haus am Pinasberg, Das; Ger, 1969; (Vohrer); Tilly Lauenstein; *MFB* 38, p. 220.
Germany in Autumn (see *Deutschland im Herbst*).
Gemany Year Zero; Fr/Ger, 1947; (Rossellini); Edmund Meschke, Ernst Pittschau; *MFB* 16, p. 87.
Geschlecht im Fesseln; Ger, 1928; (Dieterle); Paul Henckels, Hans Heinrich von Twandowski.
Getting of Wisdom, The; Austr, 1977; (Beresford); Susannah Fowle, Hilary Ryan; *MFB* 46, pp. 95–6.
Gilda; USA, 1946; (Vidor); Glenn Ford, George Macready; *MFB* 13, p. 48.
Ginger; USA, 1971; (Schain); Cheri Caffaro, Cindy Barnett; *Filmfacts* vol. XIV no 8, p. 165.
giornata particolare, Una; It/Can, 1977; (Scola); Marcello Mastroianni, Sophia Loren; *MFB* 45, p. 89.
Girl/Boy; GB, 1971; (Kellett); Joan Greenwood, Peter Straker; *MFB* 38, p. 181.
Girl called Jules, A (see *La ragazza di nome Giulio*).
Girl with Golden Eyes, The (see *La fille aux yeux d'or*).
Glass House, The; USA, 1972; (Gries); Vic Morrow, Clu Gulager; *MFB* 39, p. 250.
Gola profonda nera (Queen of Sex); It, 1976; (Moore (Zurli)); Ajita Wilson; *MFB* 46, pp. 121–2.
Goldfinger; GB, 1964; (Hamilton); Sean Connery, Honor Blackman; *MFB* 31, p. 161.
Goodbye Emmanuelle; Fr, 1977; (Leterrier); Sylvia Kristel, Alexandra Stewart; *MFB* 45, p. 24.
Goodbye Gemini; GB, 1970; (Gibson); Martin Potter, Alexis Kanner; *MFB* 37, p. 186.
Goodbye Girl, The; USA, 1977; (Ross); Richard Dreyfuss; *MFB* 45, pp. 46–7.
Good Neighbour, The (see *A Kedves Szomszéd*).
gourmandines, Les (Three into Sex won't Go); Fr, 1973; (Pérol); Sandra Julien, Jacques Cornet; *MFB* 42, p. 238.
Gringo uccidi (Django Kill); It/Sp, 1966; (Questi); Tomas Milian, Piero Lulli; Scheugl, pp. 220–1.
Group, The; USA, 1965; (Lumet); Candice Bergen, Joan Hackett; *MFB* 33, p. 163.
Groupies; USA, 1970; (Dorfman & Nevard); *MFB* 39, p. 233.
Gruppo di famiglia in un interno (Conversation Piece); It/Fr, 1974; (Visconti); Burt Lancaster, Helmut Berger; *MFB* 43, p. 28.
Guter Hahn wird selten Fett, Ein (Close Encounters of a Handyman); Ger, 1978; (Wyder); Rainer Peets, Jan Boven; *MFB* 45, p. 240.

Hard Dollar Hustler; GB, 1977; (Purnell); Joe Hill, Ken Levy; *Gay News* 133, p. 31.
Harlis (Love Me Gently); Ger, 1972; (Ackeren); Masha Rabben, Gabi Larifari; *MFB* 41 p. 126.
Harlot; USA, 1965; (Warhol); Mario Montez; *Film Culture* no. 40.
Haunting, The; GB, 1962; (Wise); Julie Harris, Claire Bloom; *MFB* 31, p. 4.
Heat; USA, 1971; (Morrissey); Joe Dallesandro, Sylvia Miles; *MFB* 40, p. 97.
Heat Wave (see *Ondate di calore*).
Here Comes Everybody; USA 1972; (Whitmore); *MFB* 40, p. 10.
Hickey and Boggs; USA, 1972; (Culp); Bill Cosby, Robert Culp; *MFB* 39, pp. 233–4.
High Infidelity (see *Alta infedelita*).
High Rise; USA; (Stone); Tamie Trevor; *S*, p. 159.
Highway Hustler; S, p. 198.
Hoera een Homo!; Neths, 1978; (van Praag).
Holding; USA, 1971; Dawson, p. 10.
Hollywood Blue; S, p. 88.
Home Movie; USA; (Oxenburg); Dawson, p. 76.
homme de désir, L'; Fr, 1970; (Delouche); François Timmerman, Eric Laborey; *MFB* 41, pp. 177–8.
Homo-actualités; Fr, 1977; (Terry); Roger Peyrefitte; *Ecran* no. 62 p. 65.
Homologues ou La soif du mâle; Fr, 1977; (Merkins (Scandelari)); *Ecran no. 65, P. 79.*
Homosexual Century, The (see *Race d'ep*).

Homosexuality and Its Problems; GB, 1977; (Medical Recording Service Foundation); *BISFA* magazine no. 57, p. 11.
Homosexuals, The; USA; (CBS).
Horse; USA, 1965; (Warhol); Gregory Battcock, Larry Latrue.
How the Hell are You?; Can; (Soul).
Huis clos; Fr, 1954; (Audry); Arletty, Gaby Sylvia; *MFB* 27, p. 3.
Hvem har bestemt . . . !?; Nor, 1978; (Vennerød); Petter Vennerød, Sossen Krohg; *Film og Kino* no. 6, p. 222.
Hrorfor goer de det? (Why?); Den, 1971; (Kronhausen); Vogel, p. 257.

I, a Man; (Warhol); *S,* p. 188.
I am a Nymphomaniac (see *Je suis une nymphomane*).
I, a Woman – 3 (see *Tre Slags Kaerlighed*).
Ich; (Junren).
Ich liebe dich, ich töte dich; Ger, 1971 (Brandner); Rolf Becker, Hannes Fuchs; Scheugl, p. 161.
I don't know; USA, 1971; (Spheeris); *Filmakers' Newsletter* vol. 4 no. 1, May 1971, p. 50.
I escaped from Devil's Island; USA, 1973; (Witney); Jim Brown, Christopher George; *MFB* 41, p. 100.
If . . . ; GB, 1968; (Anderson); Malcolm McDowell, Richard Warwick; *MFB* 36, pp. 25–6.
Ijdijk; Neths, 1963; (Seip); Scheugl, p. 281.
Ik en Charly (Me and Charly); Den, 1978; (Kristiansen).
Il était une fois dans l'est; Can, 1974; (Brassard).
Illiac Passion, The; USA, 1966; (Markopoulos); Richard Beauvais; *Film Culture* nos. 53/54/55, pp. 84–93.
Immoral Tales (see *Contes immoraux*).
I'm not one of 'em; USA, 1976; (Oxenburg); *Jump Cut* no. 20, pp. 10–11.
I'm not from here; Can, 1977; (Marks).
Imposters; USA, 1979; (Rappaport); Peter Evans, Ellen McElduff; *Variety* 21.11.79, p. 25.
In a Lonely Place; USA, 1950; (Ray); Humphrey Bogart, Gloria Grahame; *MFB* 17, p. 80.
Inadmissable Evidence; GB, 1968; (Page); Nicol Williamson, John Normington; *MFB* 36, p. 141.
In Love with Sex (see *Donnez-nous notre amour quotidien*).
Inside Daisy Clover; USA, 1965; (Mulligan); Robert Redford, Natalie Wood; *MFB* 33, p. 103.
Inside Out; GB/Ger; (Duffell); Adrian Hoven; *MFB* 42, p. 239.
Internecine Project, The; GB/Ger, 1974; (Hughes); Harry Andrews, James Coburn; *MFB* 41, p. 200.
In the Best Interests of the Children; USA, 1978; (Reid, Stevens, Zheutlin); *BNFC* 1978, vol. 16.
Intimate Confessions of a Chinese Courtesan; HK, 1973; (Yuan); Lily Ho, Betty; *MFB* 40, p. 228.
Intimate Teenage Secrets (see *It Could Happen to You*).
Investigation of Murder, An (The Laughing Policeman); USA, 1973; (Rosenberg); Walter Matthau, Bruce Dern; *MFB* 41, pp. 128–9.
In Winterlight; Can; (City Films).
Io Emmanuelle (A Man for Emmanuelle); It, 1969; (Canevari); Erika Blanc; *MFB* 37, p. 207.
Iskindiria-leh? (Alexandria — why?); Egypt/Algeria, 1978; (Chahine); Nagla Fathis, Farid Sharski; *Variety* 21.3.79, p. 26.
Isola delle Svedesi, L' (Twisted Girls); It, 1969; (Amadio); Katherine Diamant, Ewa Green; *MFB* 37, p. 130.
Isola di Arturo, L'; It, 1962; (Damiani); Reginald Kersman, Kay Meersman; *MFB* 30, p. 60.
It Could Happen to You; GB, 1975; (Long); Robert Cotton, Peter Vaughan-Clarke; *MFB* 43, p. 84.
It is not the Homosexual who is Perverse, but the Situation in which he lives (see *Nicht der Homosexuell ist pervers, sondern die Situation, in der er lebt*).

Jagdszenen aus Niederbayern; Ger, 1968; (Fleischmann); Martin Sperr, Angela Winkler; *Filmfacts* vol. 16 no. 7 pp. 174–6.

Je bent niet alleen (You are not alone); Den, 1978; (Nielsen/Johansen).
Je suis une nymphomane; Fr, 1971; (Pécas); Sandra Julien, Janine Raymond; *MFB* 38, p. 241.
Je t'aime, moi non plus; Fr. 1975; (Gainsbourg); Joe Dallesandro, Hugues Quester; *MFB* 44, p. 100.
Je tu il elle; Belg, 1974; (Akerman); Chantal Akerman, Claire Wauthion; *MFB* 46, p. 175.
La jeune fille assassinée (see *Charlotte*).
Jeunes gens pour messieurs; Fr, 1976; (Tensi); *Ecran* no. 59, p. 66.
Jill Johnston October 1975; Can, 1977; (Wazana/Armitage); *Cinéma Canada* no. 40 Sept 77, p. 57.
Johnny Minotaur; USA, 1971; (Ford); Nikos Koulizaki, Yiannis Koutsis; *Filmfacts* vol. 14 no. 21 p. 536.
Jouissances; Fr, 1977; (Lansac); Veronique Maugarski, Brigitte Lahaie; *Ecran* no. 60, pp. 70–1.
Jubilee; GB, 1978; (Jarman); Jenny Runacre, Little Nell; *MFB* 45, p. 66.
Julia (see *Es war nicht die Nachtigall*).
junge Törless, Der; Ger, 1966; (Schlöndorff); Matthieu Carrière, Bernd Tischer; *Variety* 27.4.66.
Justine de Sade (The Violation of Justine); Fr/It/Can, 1974; (Pierson); Alice Arno; *MFB* 44, p. 44.

Kaere Irene; Den, 1971; (Thomsen); Sten Kaabe, Mette Knudsen; *Variety* 17.3.71, p. 25.
Kattorna; Swed, 1965; (Carlson); Eva Dahlbeck, Isa Quensel; *Variety* 25.12.68, p. 13.
kedves Szomszéd, A (The Good Neighbour); Hung, 1979; (Kovács); László Szabó, Margit Dayka; *Variety* 28.2.79, p. 22.
Keiko; Can/Jap, 1978; (Gagnon); Janko Wakashiba, Akiko Kitabmua; *Variety* 12.9.79, p. 20.
kermesse héroique, La; Fr, 1935; (Feyder); Francoise Rosay, Louis Jouvet; *MFB* 3, p. 179.
Kid Blue; USA, 1973; (Frawley); Dennis Hopper, Warren Oates; *MFB* 41, pp. 129–130.
Killer is on the Phone, The (see *L'assassino . . . è al telefono*).
Killing of Sister George, The; GB, 1969; (Aldrich); Beryl Reid, Susanna York; *MFB* 36, pp. 92–3.
Kinder, der sich lieben; Switz, 1966; (Schneider); Scheugl, p. 281.
Kiss; USA, 1962; (Warhol); Naomi Levine, Fred Herko.
kleine Liebe, Eine; Ger, 1968; (Thiessen); Wolf von Cramer, Bernd-Otto Niederstrasser; Scheugl p. 281.
Klosterschülerinnen, Die (Sex Life in a Convent); Ger, 1971; (Schroeder); Doris Arden, Ulrich Beiger; *MFB* 40, p. 77.
Konsequenz, Die; Ger, 1977; (Petersen); Jürgen Procknow, Ernst Hannawald; *Variety* 16.11.77, p. 25.
Kremlin Letter, The; USA, 1969; (Huston); Bibi Andersson, Richard Boone; *MFB* 37, pp. 139–40.
Kvinnolek; Swed, 1967; (Nyberg); Gun Falck, Gunnila Iwansson; Scheugl, p. 287.

Lady in Cement; USA, 1968; (Douglas); Frank Sinatra, Raquel Welch; *MFB* 36, p. 33.
L.A. Plays Itself; USA, 1972; (Halsted); Fred Halsted; *Variety* 12.4.72, p. 16.
Last of Sheila, The; USA, 1973; (Ross); Richard Benjamin, Dyan Cannon; *MFB* 40, pp. 207–8.
Lavender; USA, 1971; (Jacobs/Monahan); Dawson, p. 53.
Lawrence of Arabia; GB, 1962; (Lean); Peter O'Toole, Omar Sharif; *MFB* 30, p. 17.
League of Gentlemen, The; GB, 1960; (Dearden); Jack Hawkins, Kieron Moore; *MFB* 27, p. 65.
Leather Boys, The; GB 1963; (Furie); Colin Campbell, Dudley Sutton; *MFB* 31, p. 20.
Left Handed; USA, 1972; (Dercan/Penraat); Ray Frank, Robert Rikas; *Filmfacts* vol. 16 no. 6, p. 142.
Legend of Lylah Clare, The; USA, 1968; (Aldrich); Kim Novak, Peter Finch; *MFB* 45, p. 67.
Lenny; USA, 1974; (Fosse); Dustin Hoffman, Valerie Perrine; *MFB* 42, pp. 109–10.
Lezione private (The Private Lesson); It, 1975; (de Sisti); Carroll Baker, Renzo Montagnani; *MFB* 43, p. 215.

Levensrecht; Neths, 1949; (C.O.C.).

liaisons particulières, Les; Fr, 1969; (Pécas) Astrid Frank, Nicole Debonne; *MFB* 41, p. 138.

Liberty; USA, 1929; (McCarey); Stan Laurel, Oliver Hardy; Everson, pp. 73–5.

Lickerish Quartet, The; USA/Ger/It, 1970; (Metzger); Silvano Venturelli, Frank Wolff; *S,* p. 63.

Lilith; USA, 1964; (Rossen); Warren Beatty, Jean Seberg; *MFB* 33, p. 179.

Lion in Winter, The; GB, 1968; (Harvey); Katharine Hepburn, Peter O'Toole; *MFB* 36, p. 49.

Little Big Man; USA, 1970; (Penn); Dustin Hoffman, Martin Balsam; *MFB* 38, pp. 78–9.

Lizard in a Woman's Skin, A (see *Una lucertola con la pelle di donna*).

Lodestar; S, p. 195.

Lonely Killers, The (see *Les tueurs fous*).

Lonesome Cowboys; USA, 1968; (Warhol); Viva, Eric Emerson; *MFB* 37, p. 56.

Lot in Sodom; USA, 1934; (Webber/Watson); *MFB* 43, p. 181.

Loudest Whisper, The (The Childrens's Hour); USA 1961; (Wyler); Audrey Hepburn, Shirley MacLaine; *MFB* 29, p. 123.

Love Hungry Girls (see *Les garces*).

Love in a Woman's Prison (see *Diario segreto da un carcere femminile*).

Love Machine, The; USA, 1971; (Hedley); John Phillip Law, David Hemmings; *MFB* 39, pp. 74–5.

Lovemaking; USA, 1969; (Brakhage); *Afterimage* no. 2, Autumn 1970.

Love Me Gently (see *Harlis*).

Love Me My Way; USA; (Gershuny); George Shannon, Mary Woronow; *MFB* 40, p. 79.

Love Objects; USA; (Chomont); *LFC.*

Loving Couples (see *Älskande par*).

L-Shaped Room, The; GB, 1962; (Forbes); Cicely Courtneidge, Leslie Caron; *MFB* 30, p. 3.

lucertola con la pelle di donna, Una (A Lizard in a Woman's Skin); Fr/It/Sp, 1971; (Fulci); Florinda Bolkan, Jean Sorel; *MFB* 40, p. 150.

Ludwig; Ger/Fr/It, 1973; (Visconti); Helmut Berger, Romy Schneider; *Variety* 21.2.73, p. 18.

Ludwig II – Requiem für einen jungfräulichen König; Ger, 1972; (Syberberg); Harry Baer, Ingrid Caven; *MFB* 44, p. 46.

Lulu; USA, 1977; (Chase); Elisa Leonelli; *Variety* 24.5.78, p. 27.

Lust and Desire (see *Le désir et la volupté*).

Lust for a Vampire; GB, 1970; (Sangster); Barbara Jefford, Suzanna Leigh; *MFB* 38, p. 25.

Mädchen in Uniform; Ger, 1931; (Sagan); Dorothea Wieck, Hertha Thiele; *Women & Film* vol. 2 no. 7 Summer 75, pp. 68–71.

Mädchen in Uniform; Ger, 1958; (Radranyi); Lilli Palmer, Romy Schneider; *Variety* 16.7.58.

Maltese Falcon, The; USA, 1941; (Huston); Peter Lorre, Sidney Greenstreet; *MFB* 9, p. 46.

Manhattan; USA, 1979; (Allen); Meryl Streep, Karen Ludwig; *MFB* 46, p. 179.

Manji (All Mixed Up) (Passion); Jap, 1964; (Masumura); Ayako Wakao, Kyoko Kishida; *MFB* 34, p. 76.

Man who Fell to Earth, The; GB, 1976; (Roeg); David Bowie, Buck Henry; *MFB* 43, p. 86.

Marcados para viver; Braz, 1976; (de Rosario); Tessy Callado, Rose Lacretu; *NYFWF* p. 20.

Marco di Rio; (Rocco); *S,* p. 188.

mare, Il; It, 1962; (Griffi); Umberto Orsini, Dino Mele; *MFB* 31, p. 52.

M.A.S.H.; USA, 1969; (Altman); Donald Sutherland, John Schuck; *MFB* 37, pp.140–1.

Master Piece, The; (Friedman); *S,* p. 43.

Meat Rack; USA, 1970; (Thomas); David Calder, Donna Troy; *Variety* 15.3.70, p. 22.

meilleure façon de marcher, La; Fr, 1975; (Miller); Patrick Dewaere, Patrick Bauchitey; *MFB* 44, pp. 149–50.

Mélodrame; Fr, 1976; (Georges); Martine Simonet, Vincente Criado; *Variety* 19.5.76; p. 27.

Michael, Angelo and David; Mandate February 1977.

Midnight Cowboy; USA, 1969; (Schlesinger); Jon Voight, Dustin Hoffman; *MFB* 37, pp. 7–8.

Midnight Express; GB, 1978; (Parker); Brad Davis, Norbert Weisser; *MFB* 45, p. 139.

Midnight Geisha Boy; S, p. 191.

Mikael; Ger, 1924; (Dreyer); Benjamin Christensen, Walter Slezak; *Sight and Sound* Autumn 1965, p. 167 ff.

Milestones; USA, 1975; (Kramer/Douglas); Grace Paley, Mary Chapelle; *MFB* 44, pp. 169–70.

mille et une perversions de Felicia, Les; Fr, 1975; (Pécas); Rebecca Brooke, Jean Roche; *MFB* 43, p. 194.

Mimi la douce; S, p. 78.

Miss Leslie's Dolls; USA; (Prieto); Salvador Ugarte, Terry Juston; *MFB* 40, p. 128.

Mona: the Virgin Nymph; USA, 1970; (Osco); Fifi Watson; *S,* pp. 124–5.

Mondo Rocco; (Rocco); *S,* p. 111.

Montreal Main; Can, 1974; (Vitale); Tony Booth, Nye Maciukas; *MFB* 45, p. 222.

More, More, More; USA, 1976; (Potts); Bill Young, Darby Lloyd Rains; *Ecran* no. 55, p. 57.

Morte a Venezia (Death in Venice); It/Fr, 1971; (Visconti); Dirk Bogarde, Björn Andresen; *MFB* 38, pp. 80–1.

Music Lovers, The; GB, 1970; (Russell); Richard Chamberlain, Christopher Gable; *MFB* 38, p. 53.

My Body Burns (see *L'érotisme a l'étude*).

My Hustler; USA, 1965; (Warhol/Wein); Paul America, Ed Hood; *MFB* 38, p. 123.

Myra Breckinridge; USA, 1970; (Sarne); Raquel Welch, Mae West; *MFB* 38, p. 54.

My Tale is Hot; (Friedman); *S,* p. 43.

Naked are the Cheaters; USA, 1971; (Ashburne); Vickie Carbe, Heidi Stohler; *MFB* 42, p. 111.

Narcissus; USA, 1956; (Maas/Moore); Ben Moore, Marie Menken; Scheugl, p. 269.

Nattlek; Swed, 1966; (Zetterling); Keve Hjelm, Ingrid Thulin; *MFB* 34, pp. 24–5.

New Face in Hell (P.J.); USA, 1967; (Guillermin); George Peppard, Gayle Hunnicutt; *MFB* 35, p. 60.

New Romance – New Aspects of Sexuality and Sexual Roles; Can, 1975; (Walezeuski/Gabori).

New York City Inferno; Fr, 1978; (Markin); Christopher Dock, Bob Bleecker; *Ecran* no. 71, p. 75.

Nicht der Homosexuell ist pervers, sondern die Situation, in der er lebt; Ger, 1971; (von Praunheim); Vogel, p. 246.

Night at Joanni's, A; (Rocco); *S,* p. 188.

Night Games (see *Nattlek*).

Nighthawks; GB, 1978; (Peck/Hallam); Ken Robertson, Tony Westrope; *MFB* 46, p. 30.

Night Heat (see *La notte brava*).

Night Moves; New Zealand, 1979; (Turner); *Variety* 4.7.79.

Night Scandal in Japan (see *Akujo*).

Nights in Black Leather; (Rutkowski); Peter Berlin; *S,* p. 196.

Nikolai Stavrogin; Russia, 1915; (Protazanov); *Ocherki,* p. 20.

noms du père, Les; (Herré).

Norman Is That You?; USA, 1976; (Schlatter); Redd Foxx, Pearl Bailey; *MFB* 44, p. 47.

notte brava, La; It, 1960; (Bolignini); Laurent Terzieff, Jean-Claude Brialy;; *MFB* 27, p. 165.

Nous étions un seul homme; Fr, 1979; (Vallois).

Nous irons tous au paradis (Pardon Mon Affaire, Too); Fr, 1977; (Robert); Claude Brasseur; *MFB* 45, p. 223.

No Way to Treat a Lady; USA, 1968; (Smight); Rod Steiger, Lee Remick; *MFB* 35, p. 87.

nuit américaine, La (Day for Night); Fr/It, 1973; (Truffaut); Jacqueline Bisset, Jean-Pierre Aumont; *MFB* 41, p. 12.

Nun, The (see *La réligieuse*).

Ode to Billy Joe; USA, 1976; (Baer); Robby Benson, Glynnis O'Connor; *MFB* 43, p. 169.

oiseaux vont mourir au Pérou, Les; Fr, 1968; (Gary); Jean Seberg, Danielle Darrieux; *MFB* 35, p. 149.

Okasareta byakui (Violated Angels); Jap, 1967; (Wakamatsu); *MFB* 44, pp. 151–2.

Olga's Girls; USA; (Mawra); *S,* p. 24.

Olga's Massage Parlour; USA; (Mawra); *S,* p. 24.

Olivia; Fr, 1950; (Audry); Edwige Feuillère, Simone Simon; *MFB* 19, p. 106.

Oltre il bene e il male; It/Fr/Ger, 1977; (Cavani); Dominique Sanda, Robert Powell; *Variety* 12.10.77, p. 17.
Once is not Enough; USA, 1974; (Green); Alexis Smith, Melina Mercouri; *MFB* 42, p. 176.
Once upon a time in the East (see *Il était une fois dans l'est*).
Ondate di calore (Heat Wave); It, 1972; (Risi); Jean Seberg; *Filmfacts* vol. 14 no. 3, p. 307.
One; Mandate February 1977.
Original Pat Rocco Male Film Festival, The; (Rocco); *S*, p. 111.
Oscar Wilde; GB, 1960; (Ratoff); Robert Morley, John Neville; *MFB* 27, p. 93.
Other Sex, The (see *Equilibrium*).
Other Side of Joey, The; USA, 1972; (Hall/Marks); Erik Kahnler, Gordon Harris; *Variety* 16.8.72, p. 28.
Oublier Venise; Fr/It, 1979; (Brusati); Erland Josephson, Mariangela Melato; *Variety* 23.1.80, p. 26.
Outback; Austr, 1970; (Kotcheff); Donald Pleasance, Gary Bond; *MFB* 38, p. 244.
Outrageous!; Can, 1977; (Benner); Hollis McLaren, Craig Russell; *MFB* 45, pp. 203–4.
Ovoce stromj rajskych jime (We May Eat of the Fruit of the Trees of the Garden); Czech/Belg, 1970; (Chytilova); Jitka Norakova, Jan Schmind; Scheugl, p. 170.

Pandora's Box (see *Die Büchse der Pandora*).
Papillon; USA, 1973; (Schaffner); Dustin Hoffman, Robert Deman; *MFB* 41, p. 51.
Passionate Desires (see *Fuego*).
Pat Rocco Dares; (Rocco); *S*, p. 111.
Paul and David; Can, 1979; (Lemmon/Sutherland).
Pawnbroker, The; USA, 1963; (Lumet); Rod Steiger, Brock Peters; *MFB* 33, p. 181.
Pecado mortal (Mortal Sin); Braz, 1970; (Faria); Jose Lergoy, Fernando Montenegro; *Variety* 9.9.70, p. 22.
Performance; GB, 1970; (Cammell/Roeg); Mick Jagger, James Fox; *MFB* 38, p. 27.
Perrak; Ger, 1970; (Vohrer); Horst Tappert, Walter Richter; Scheugl, p. 290.
Pete 'n' Tillie; USA, 1972; (Ritt); Walter Matthau, Rene Auberjonois; *MFB* 40, p. 81.
Persona; Swed, 1965; (Bergman); Bibi Andersson, Liv Ullmann; *MFB* 34, p. 169.
Personals; USA; (Weston/Winters); *S*, p. 89.
pianos mecaniques, Les; Fr/Sp, 1964; (Bardem); Melina Mercouri, James Mason; *Variety* 26.5.65.
Piggies; Ger, 1970; (Zadek); *Variety* 20.5.70, p. 28.
Pink Flamingoes; USA, 1973; (Waters); Divine, David Lochary; *MFB* 45, pp.11–12.
Pink Narcissus; USA, 1971; (–); Bobby Kendall; *S*, pp. 190–1.
Pink Panther Strikes Again, The; GB, 1976; (Edwards); Peter Sellers, Michael Robbins; *MFB* 44, p. 29.
P.J. (see *New Face in Hell*).
Place between our Bodies, The; USA; (Wallin).
Play It as it Lays; USA, 1972; (Perry); *Filmfacts* vol. XV no. 20, pp. 494–7.
Pleasure Cruise, The; S, p. 191.
Pleasure Girls, The; GB, 1965; (O'Hara); Francesca Annis, Ian McShane; *MFB* 32, p. 112.
Pledgemaster, The; USA, 1971; (Halsted); *S*, p. 193.
Pool Party; Sexuality in the Movies, p. 161.
Pornography in Hollywood; (Kirkland); *S*, p. 93.
Portrait; GB, 1977; (Jackson); Monica Sjöo.
Portrait of Jason; USA, 1967; (Clarke); Jason Holliday; *MFB* 45, p. 51.
Position of Faith, A; USA, 1973; (Rhodes); William Johnson; *BNFC* vol. 10.
Possession du condamné; Belg, 1967; (Lheureux); Luc Alesandre, Gilles Brenta; Scheugl, p. 278.
Pourquoi pas?; Fr, 1977; (Serreau); Sami Frey, Mario Gonzales; *Variety* 14.12.77, p. 12.
Prazké Noci (Prague Nights); Czech/Pol, 1969; (Schorm); Jana Brezkova, Tereza Tuszynska; Scheugl, p. 170.
Precinct 45 – Los Angeles Police; USA, 1972; (Fleischer); George C. Scott, Stacy Keach; *MFB* 39, p. 257.

Prey; GB, 1977; (Warren); Glory Annen, Sally Faulkner; *MFB* 45, p. 119.
primo premio si chiami Irene, Il (First Prize Irene); It, 1969; (Ragazzi); *MFB* 38, p. 169.
Prison Girls; USA, 1973; (de Simone); *MFB* 41, pp. 154–5.
Private Lesson, The (see *Lezione Private*).
Private Files of J. Edgar Hoover, The; USA, 1977; (Cohen); Broderick Crawford, Dan Dailey; *MFB* 46, pp. 30–1.
Producers, The; USA, 1967, (Brooks); Zero Mostel, Gene Wilder; *MFB* 36, p. 233.
Pursuit of Happiness, The; USA, 1970; (Mulligan); Michael Sarrazin, Ralph Waite; *MFB* 41, p. 183.

Quai des Orfèvres; Fr, 1947; (Clouzot); Louis Jouvet, Simone Renart; *MFB* 15, p. 6.
Queen, The; USA, 1968; (Simon); Crystal, Harlow; *MFB* 36, p. 39.
Queen of Sex (see *Gola profonda nera*).
Queerdom; USA; (Kim/Gifford); animation; *GN* 157, p. 38.
Queer . . . the Erotic, The (see *L'altra faccia del peccato*).

Race d'ep (The Homosexual Century); Fr, 1979; (Soukaz/Hocquenghem); Elizar von Effenterre, Pierre Hahn; *Variety* 5.3.80, p. 22.
Rachel, Rachel; USA, 1967; (Newman); Joanne Woodward, Estelle Parsons; *MFB* 35, p. 174.
ragazza di nome Giulio, La (A Girl called Jules); It, 1970; (Valerii); Silvia Dionisio, Anna Moffo; *MFB* 42, p. 160.
ragazzi del massacro, I (Sex in the Classroom); It, 1969 (Leo); Pier Paolo Capponi, Susan Scott; *MFB* 39, p. 14.
Rainbow's Children; 1974; (Williams).
rainha diaba, A (Devil Queen); Braz, 1975; (Foutoura); Milton Goncalves, Odette Lara; *Variety* 1.10.75, p. 28.
Reach for Glory; GB, 1966; (Leacock); Harry Andrews, Kay Walsh; *MFB* 29, p. 169.
Rebecca; USA, 1940; (Hitchcock); Joan Fontaine, Judith Anderson; *MFB* 7, p. 115.
Rebel without a Cause; USA, 1955; (Ray); James Dean, Sal Mineo; *MFB* 23, p. 17.
Redeemer, The; USA, 1976; (Gochis); Michael Hollingsworth, Gyr Pattison; *MFB* 45, pp. 119–20.
Reflections in a Golden Eye; USA, 1967; (Huston); Marlon Brando, Robert Forster; *MFB* 35, p. 114.
règle du jeu, La; Fr, 1938–9; (Renoir); Marcel Dalio, Gaston Modot; *MFB* 28, p. 152.
religieuse, La (The Nun); Fr, 1965; (Rivette); Anna Karina, Liselotte Pulver; *MFB* 34, p. 171.
rempart des béguines, Le; Fr; (Casaril).
Requiem a l'aube; Fr, 1977; (Desbordes); Patrice Gouron, Didier Silhiol; *Ecran* no. 57, p. 70.
révélation, La; Fr, 1971; (Lavalle); *MFB* 40, p. 195.
Richard; (Beauvais).
Riot; USA, 1968; (Kulik); Jim Brown, Gene Hackman; *MFB* 36, p. 149.
Ritual of Blood (see *Ceremonia sangrieta*).
Ritz, The; GB, 1975; (Lester); Jack Weston, Rita Moreno; *MFB* 43, p. 255.
Robert Having his Nipple Pierced; GB, 1971; (Daley); *BNFC* Sept 71.
Robin Crusoe; S, p. 78.
Rocco e i suoi fratelli; It, 1960; (Visconti); Renato Salvatori, Roger Hanin; *MFB* 28, p. 152.
Rocky Horror Picture Show, The; GB, 1975; (Sharman); Tim Curry, Peter Hinwood; *MFB* 42, p. 181.
Rollin' with love; Jump Cut no. 20, p. 10.
Roma città aperta; It, 1945; (Rossellini); Anna Magnani, Aldo Fabrizi; *MFB* 14, p. 102.
Rope; USA, 1948; (Hitchcock); Farley Granger, John Dall; *MFB* 15, p. 176.
Rose, The; USA, 1979; (Rydell); Bette Midler, Sandra McCabe; *MFB* 47, pp. 11–12.
Rosebud; USA, 1974; (Preminger); Peter O'Toole, Richard Attenborough; *MFB* 42, p. 87.
rouge aux lèvres, Le (Daughters of Darkness); Belg/Fr/Ger/It, 1970; (Kümel); Delphine Seyrig, Danièle Ouimet; *MFB* 38, p. 203.
Rubber Gun; Can, 1977; (Moyle/Lack); *Variety* 31.8.77, p. 19.

Sado; Jap, 1978; (Higashi); Toshiyuki Nagashima, Chiyoko Shimagura; *Variety* 11.10.78, p. 48.
Salo; It/Fr, 1975; (Pasolini); Paolo Bonacelli, Giorgio Cataldi; *MFB* 46, pp. 200–1.
Sandy and Madeline's Family; USA; (Farrell/Bruce/Hill); Dawson, p. 35.
Sappho Darling; USA, 1969; (Steele); Carole Young, Yvonne d'Angers; *Variety* 12.3.69, p. 6.
Satana Likuyushchii (Satan Triumphing); Russia, ?1916; (Protazanov); *Ocherki,* p. 20.
Satan bouch un coin; (Bouyxou).
Satansbraten (Satan's Brew); Ger, 1976; (Fassbinder); Kurt Raab; *MFB* 47, p. 27.
Saturday Night at the Baths; USA, 1974; (Buckley); Robert Aberdeen, Don Scotti; *MFB* 43, p. 173.
Satyricon; It, 1969; (Fellini); Martin Potter, Hiram Keller; *MFB* 37, p. 200.
Says Who . . . !? (see *Hvem har bestent . . . !?*).
Scarecrow; USA, 1973; (Schatzberg); Gene Hackman, Al Pacino; *MFB* 40, p. 212.
Schemerhoorn; Neths, 1966; (Seip); Scheugl, p. 281.
School Girl; USA, 1971; (Gerber); *S,* p. 130.
Schwestern der Revolution; Ger, 1969/70; (von Praunheim); *F & F* vol. 16 no. 8, p. 88.
Score; USA/Yug, 1973; (Metzger); Calvin Culver, Claire Wilbur; *S,* p. 63.
Scorpio Rising; USA, 1963; (Anger); Bruce Byron, Johnny Sapienza; *MFB* 32, p. 172.
Scum; GB, 1979; (Clarke); Ray Winstone, Julian Firth; *MFB* 46, pp. 201–2.
Sebastiane; GB, 1976; (Jarman); Leonardo Treviglio, Barney James; *MFB* 43, p. 235.
Sekstet; Den, 1963; (Hovmand); Ingrid Thulin, Ghita Norby; *F & F* March 1964, p. 47.
Sensuous Doll (see *Les confidences de Sandra*).
Sentinel, The; USA, 1976; (Winner); *MFB* 44, pp. 51–2.
Sergeant, The; USA, 1968; (Flynn); Rod Steiger, John Philip Law; *MFB* 36, p. 60.
Servant, The; GB, 1963; (Losey); Dirk Bogarde, James Fox; *MFB* 30, p. 169.
Seven in a Barn; (Brian); *S,* p. 195.
Seven Women; USA, 1966; (Ford); Margaret Leighton, Anne Bancroft; *MFB* 34, p. 6.
Seventh Victim, The; USA, 1943; (Robson); Kim Hunter, Evelyn Brent; *MFB* 46, p. 82.
Sex and the Single Gay; (Rocco); *S,* p. 111.
Sex and the Vampire (see *Le frisson des vampires*).
sexe des anges, La; (Soukar).
Sex Garage, The; USA; (Halsted); *S,* p. 193.
Sex in the Classroom (see *I ragazzi del massacro*).
Sex is Beautiful (see *La révélation*).
Sex Life in a Convent (see *Die Klosterschülerinnen*).
Sex Nest, The (see *Das gelbe Haus aus Pinasberg*).
Sexpert, The; USA, 1976; (Sarno); Rebecca Brooke, Sarah Nicholson; *MFB* 46, pp. 153–4.
Sex Shop; Fr/It/Ger, 1972; (Berri); Jean-Pierre Marielle, Juliet Berto; *MFB* 40, pp. 105–6.
Sextrovert, The (see *Desirella*).
Sexual Desire; USA, 1974; (Peeters/Deerson); Elizabeth Plume, Jon Aprea; *MFB* 42, p. 116.
Sexus; (Benazeraf); *S,* p. 51.
Sexy Lovers (see *La chatte sans pudeur*).
Shark's Treasure; USA, 1974; (Wilde); Cornel Wilde, Cliff Osmond; *MFB* 42, p. 269.
Sheila Levine is Dead and Living in New York; USA, 1975; (Furie); Jeannie Berlin, Roy Scheider; *Variety* 5.2.75, p. 20.
Short Eyes; USA, 1977; (Young); Bruce Davison, Shawn Elliott; *MFB* 45, pp. 206–7.
Sidelong Glances of a Pigeon Kicker; USA, 1970; (Dexter); Jordan Christopher, Robert Walden; *MFB* 39, pp. 145–6.
Sign of the Cross; USA, 1932; (De Mille); Charles Laughton, Claudette Colbert.
Silence, The (see *Tystnaden*).
Sisters!; USA, 1973 (Hammer); Dawson, p. 46.
Sisters of the Revolution (see *Schwestern der Revolution*).
Slaves; USA, 1973; (Meyer); Anouska Hempel, Bernard Boston; *MFB* 45, p. 54.
Sodom and Gomorrah; It/Fr, 1962; (Aldrich/Leone); Stewart Granger, Anouk Aimée; *MFB* 29, p. 174.
Sodom and Gomorrah; USA, 1976; (Mitchells); Sean Brancato, Deborah Brast; *Variety* 3.3.76, p. 39.

So Evil So Young; GB, 1960; (Grayson); Jill Ireland, Ellen Pollock; *MFB* 28, p. 99.
So Long Blue Boy; USA, 1973; (Gordon); Arthur Franz, Rick Gates; *Variety* 28.11.73, p. 16.
Some Call It Loving; USA, 1973; (Harris); Carol White, Tisa Farrow; *MFB* 42, pp. 182–3.
Some of My Best Friends Are . . .; USA, 1971; (Nelson); Tom Bade, David Baker; *MFB* 39, pp. 36–7.
Some of Your Best Friends; USA, 1972; (Robinson); *GN* 8.
Someone; USA, 1968; (Rocco); Joe Adair, Bambi Allen; *Variety* 11.12.68, p. 32.
Something for Everyone (see *Black Flowers for the Bride*).
Song of the Loon; USA, 1970; (Herbert); *S*, p. 189.
Son of the Family, A; Can, 1977; (Selway/McMaster Film Board).
sovversivi, I; It, 1967; (Taviani); Marija Tozinowsky, Fabienne Fabre; *Variety* 4.10.67, p. 16.
Spartacus; USA, 1960; (Kubrick); Laurence Olivier, Tony Curtis; *MFB* 28, p. 6.
Special Day, A (see *Una giornata particolare*).
Splendori e miserie di Madame Royale; It, 1970; (Caprioli); Ugo Tognazzi, Vittorio Caprioli; Scheugl, p. 258.
Staircase; GB, 1969; (Donen); Rex Harrison, Richard Burton; *MFB* 36, p. 260–1.
Stamen; USA, 1972; (Beeson); Dawson, p. 10.
stances à Sophie, Les; Can, 1970; (Mizraki); Michel Duchaussoy, Bernadette Lafont; *Women & Film* no.1, p. 69.
Sticks and Stones; USA, 1970; (Lo Presto); Craig Dudley, J. Will Deane; *Variety* 28.1.70, p. 17.
Stewardesses, The; USA, 1970; (Silliman); Christina Hart, Angelique de Moline; *MFB* 41, p. 34.
Stop It – I Like It (see *Alpenglühn im Dirndlrock*).
Story of Joanna, The; USA, 1975; (Damiano); James Gillis, Terri Hall; *MFB* 44, pp. 153–4.
Strange Lovers; USA, 1963; (Stambler); Walter Koenig, Jo d'Agosta; *Variety* 10.7.63.
Strangers on a Train; USA, 1951; (Hitchcock); Robert Walker, Farley Granger; *MFB* 18, p. 309.
Studenthotel von St. Pauli, Das; Ger, 1970; (Olson); Curt Jürgens, Michael Maien; Scheugl, pp. 160–1.
Suddenly Last Summer; USA, 1957; (Mankiewicz); Elizabeth Taylor, Montgomery Clift; *MFB* 27, p. 81.
Summer Wishes, Winter Dreams; USA, 1973; (Cates); Joanne Woodward, Martin Balsam; *MFB* 41, p. 54.
Sunday Bloody Sunday; GB, 1971; (Schlesinger); Peter Finch, Murray Head; *MFB* 38, pp. 146–7.
Suor Emmanuelle (Sister Emmanuelle); It, 1977; (Vari); Laura Gemser, Monika Zanchi; *MFB* 47, p. 53.
Suzy Chalk; GB, 1974; (Bradford).
Sylvia; USA, 1964; (Douglas); Carroll Baker, Joanna Dru; *MFB* 32, p. 89.
Symptoms; GB, 1974; (Larraz); Angela Pleasance, Lorna Heilbron; *MFB* 43, p. 153.

Tabu; Swed, 1977; (Sjöman); Kjell Bergquist; *F & F* vol. 24 no. 2, p. 28.
Tamarind Seed, The GB, 1974; (Edwards); Julie Andrews, Omar Sharif; *MFB* 41, p. 159.
Taste of Honey, A; GB, 1962; (Richardson); Rita Tushingham, Murray Melvin; *MFB* 28, p. 140.
Tea and Sympathy; USA, 1956; (Minnelli); John Kerr, Deborah Kerr; *MFB* 24, p. 85.
Teenage Hitchikers; USA, 1974; (Sedley); Kathie Christopher, Sandra Peabody; *MFB* 44, p. 216.
Tell Me that You Love Me, Junie Moon; USA, 1969; (Preminger); Liza Minnelli, Robert Moore; *MFB* 38, p. 84.
10; USA, 1980; (Edwards); Julie Andrews, Dudley Moore; *MFB* 47, pp. 12–13.
Tenderness of Wolves, The (see *Die Zärtlichkeit der Wölfe*).
Teorema; It, 1968; (Pasolini); Terence Stamp, Silvana Mangano; *MFB* 36, pp. 96–7.
Thanos and Despina; Gr, 1968; (Papatakis); *Mandat* Jan. 1977.

That Certain Summer; USA, 1973; (Johnson); Hal Holbrook, Hope Lange; *Film Quarterly* vol. 26 no. 4 p. 63.

Theatre of Blood; GB, 1973; (Hickox); Vincent Price, Diana Rigg; *MFB* 40, p. 132.

Thérèse (Thérèse Desqueyroux); Fr, 1962; (Franju); Emmanuelle Riva; *MFB* 32, p. 36.

Thérèse and Isabelle; USA/Ger, 1968; (Metzger); Essy Persson, Anna Gael; *MFB* 36, p. 199.

There was a Crooked Man; USA, 1969; (Mankiewicz); Kirk Douglas, Hume Cronyn; *MFB* 37, pp. 247–8.

They Only Kill their Masters; USA, 1972; (Goldstone); James Garner, June Allyson; *MFB* 40, p. 155.

Third Sex, The (see *Anders als Du und Ich*).

This Sporting Life; GB, 1968; (Anderson); William Hartnell, Richard Harris; *MFB* 30, p. 35.

Three Forbidden Stories (see *Tre storie proibite*).

Three into Sex won't go (see *Les gourmandines*).

Three Lives; USA, 1970; (Millett/Irvine/Mide/Klechner); Robin Mide; *Filmfacts* vol. 14 no. 24, p. 750.

Three Strange Loves (see *Törst*).

Thundercrack; USA, 1975; (McDowell).

To an Unknown God (see *A un dios desconocido*).

Tod der Maria Malibrau, Der; Ger, 1971; (Schroeber); Vogel, pp. 69–70.

To Forget Venice (see *Oublier Venise*).

Tommy; GB, 1975; (Russell); Keith Moon, Roger Daltrey; *MFB* 42, p. 88.

Tony Rome; USA, 1967; (Douglas); Frank Sinatra, Jill St. John; *MFB* 35, p. 24.

Törst; Swed, 1949; (Bergman); Mimi Nelson, Eva Henning.

Toute une vie (And now my Love); Fr/It, 1974; (Lelouche); Marthe Keller, Andre Dussollier; *MFB* 42, p. 145.

Town Bloody Hall; USA, 1979; (Pennebaker); Jill Johnston: *MFB* 47, pp. 53–4.

Traitement de choc (Doctor in the Nude); Fr/It, 1972; (Jessua); Alain Delon, Robert Hirsch; *MFB* 42, pp. 63–4.

Trash; USA, (Morrissey); Joe Dallesandro; *MFB* 40, p. 38.

Tre Slags Kaerlighed (I – A Woman, 3); Den, 1970; (Ahlberg); Gun Falck, Inger Sundh; *MFB* 38, p. 185.

Tre Storie proibite; It, 1952; (Genina); Isa Pola, Antonella Lualdi; *MFB* 20, p. 51.

Trials of Oscar Wilde; GB, 1960; (Hughes); Peter Finch, John Fraser; *MFB* 27, p. 95.

Trick and Trade; S, p. 189.

Trotta; Ger, 1971; (Scharf); Andras Balint, Rosemarie Fendel; *Variety* 8.12.71, p. 20/4.

Truxx; Can, 1978; (Sutherland).

tueurs fous, Les; Belg, 1972; (Szulzeuger); Roland Maden, Dominique Rollin; *Cinéma 72* no. 168, p. 152.

Turning Point, The; USA, 1977; (Ross); Shirley MacLaine, Daniel Levans; *MFB* 45, pp. 73–4.

Twee Vrowen (Twice a Woman); Neths, 1979; (Sluizer); Bibi Andersson, Sandra Dumas; *Variety* 16.5.79, p. 35.

Twice a Man; USA, 1963; (Markopoulos); Olympia Dukakis, Paul Kilb; *Film Culture* Winter 63–64, p. 10.

Twice a Woman (see *Twee Vrowen*).

Twilight Cowboy; S, p. 191.

Twilight Girls, The (see *Les collégiennes*).

Twins of Evil; GB, 1971; (Hough); Madeleine Collinson, Mary Collinson; *MFB* 38, p. 226.

Twisted Girls (see *L'isola delle Svedesi*).

Two Gentlemen Sharing; GB, 1968; (Kotcheff); Judy Geeson, Robin Phillips; *Variety* 10.9.69, p. 36.

Tystnaden; Swed, 1962; (Bergman); Ingrid Thulin, Gunnel Lindblom; *MFB* 31, p. 91.

Uden en Traevel (Without a Stitch); Den, 1968; (Meineche); Anne Grete, Joan Gamst; *MFB* 38, p. 60.

Under the Bed; GB, 1976; (Grant); John Hamill, Theresa Wood; *MFB* 44, p. 54.

Unmarried Woman, An; USA, 1977; (Mazursky); Jill Clayburgh, Penelope Russianoff; *MFB* 45, p. 144.
Up the Chastity Belt; GB, 1971; (Kellett); Frankie Howerd, Anna Quayle; *MFB* 39, pp. 17–18.

Valentino; GB, 1977; (Russell); Rudolph Nureyev; *MFB* 44, pp. 244–5.
Vampire Lovers, The; GB, 1970; (Baker); Ingrid Pitt, Pippa Steele; *MFB* 37, pp. 207–8.
Vampyres; GB, 1975; (Larraz); Marianne Morris, Anulka; *MFB* 43, p. 132.
Velvet Vampire, The; USA, 1971; (Rothman); Michael Blodgett, Sherry Miles; *Filmfacts* vol. 14 no. 20, pp. 500–2.
Venusberg; Ger, 1964; (Seitz); Marissa Mell, Nicole Radal; *Variety* 22.4.64.
Very Natural Thing, A; USA, 1974; (Larkin); Robert Joel, Curt Gareth; *Variety* 29.5.74, p. 14.
Victim; GB, 1961; (Dearden); Dirk Bogarde, Peter McEnery; *MFB* 28, p. 126.
Violated Angels (see *Okasaretu Byakui*).
Vir Amat; Can.
Villain; GB, 1971; (Tuchner); Richard Burton, Ian McShane; *MFB* 38, pp. 149–50.
Virgin Lovers (see *L'amour humain*).
Virgin Soldiers; GB, 1968; (Dexter); Lynn Redgrave, Wayne Sleep; *MFB* 36, pp. 261–2.
Virgin Witch; GB 1970; (Austin); Ann Michelle, Vicky Michelle; *MFB* 39, p. 60.
vitelloni, I; It, 1953; (Fellini); Alberto Sordi, Franco Interlenghi; *MFB* 23, p. 59.
Vixen; (Meyer); Erica Gavin, Vincene Wallace; *S*, p. 62.

Walk on the Wild Side, A; USA, 1962; (Dmytryk); Barbara Stanwyck, Capucine; *MFB* 29, p. 55.
Warlock; USA, 1959; (Dmytryk); Richard Widmark, Anthony Quinn; *MFB* 26, p. 69.
Way of the Dragon, The; HK, 1973; (Lee); Bruce Lee; *MFB* 41, p. 110.
We May Eat the Fruit of the Trees of the Garden (see *Ovoce stromj rajskych jime*).
We're Alive; USA, 1976; (Women's Film Workshop of UCLA).
We're not Afraid Any More; 1974,
What About McBride; USA, 1974.
White Slaves of Chinatown; USA; (Mawra); *S*, p. 24.
Why? (see *Hrorfor goer de det?*).
Wild Geese, The; GB, 1977; (McLaglen); Richard Burton, Kenneth Griffith; *MFB* 45, pp. 145–6.
Wild in the Sky; USA, 1971; (Naud); Brandon de Wilde, Robert Lansing; *MFB* 39, pp. 261–2.
Windows; USA, 1980.
Without a Stitch (see *Uden en Traevel*).
Woman Hunt (see *Au royaume des cieux*).
Woman Needs Loving, A (see *Eine Frau sucht Liebe*).
Woman's Place is in the Home, A; USA, 1975; (Porter/Lemle); Elaine Noble; *Jump Cut* no. 20, p. 9.
Women in Cages; USA, 1971; (de Leon); Jennifer Gan, Judy Brown; *Filmfacts* vol. 14, p. 703.
Women in Love; GB, 1969; (Russell); Alan Bates, Oliver Reed; *MFB* 36, pp. 263–4.
Women's Happy Time Commune; (Page); *Jump Cut* no. 20, pp. 9–11.
Word is Out; USA, 1977; (Mariposa Film Group); *MFB* 45, p. 228.
World Ten Times Over, The; GB, 1963; (Rilla); Sylvia Syms, June Ritchie; *MFB* 30, p. 156.
W.R. – Misterje Organizma; Ger/Yug, 1971; (Makavejev); Milena Dravić, Jackie Curtis; *MFB* 39, pp. 19–20.

Yes; USA, 1969; *Mandate* Feb. 1977.
You Can't have Everything (Cactus in the Snow); USA, 1970; (Zweiback); Richard Thomas, Mary Layne; *MFB* 38, pp. 61–2.
You Can't Run Away from Sex; USA; 1971; (Webber); William Smith, Gilda Texter; *MFB* 39, p. 219.
Young Törless (see *Der jung Törless*).

Z; Fr/Algeria, 1968; (Costa-Gavras); Yves Montand, Jean-Louis Trintignant; *MFB* 36, pp. 238–9.
Zärtlichkeit der Wölf; Ger, 1973; (Lommel); Kurt Raab, Jeff Roden; *MFB* 43, p. 133.
Zéro de conduite; Fr, 1933; (Vigo); Jean Daste, Obert Le Flon; *MFB* 13, p. 127.

Bibliography

I have not attempted anything like a comprehensive up-date of this bibliography since the first edition. There has been a considerable growth in film criticism in the gay press, much of it of a high quality (e.g. Jack Babuscio, Lee Atwell, Tom Waugh, Robin Wood – I am not aware of any lesbian critics regularly in the gay press). To include every such example would extend this bibliography inordinately, and rather than make invidious judgements as to 'lasting merit', I have restricted entries to pieces dealing at some length with a general topic (including the work of particular directors, actors, etc.) – in other words, I have not included reviews of single films, however thoughtful or important.

Atwell, Lee, 'Homosexual Themes in the Cinema', *Tangents*, 1 (6), Mar 66, pp. 4–10; 1 (7), Apr 66, pp. 4–9; 'Visconti', *Gay Sunshine*, 29/30; 'The films of Pasolini', *Gay Sunshine* 28.

Babsucio, Jack: articles in *Gay News* – 73 (gay men and 'camp women'), 74 (John Schlesinger), 75 (images of 'masculinity'), 76 (hardporn), 78 (censorship), 79 (James Dean), 80 (Parker Tyler), 81 (sexual colonialism in the British cinema), 83 (repression and role-playing), 85 (Marilyn Monroe), 86 (gays and the military in film), 87 (Andy Warhol), 88 (Paul Morrissey), 89 (Oscar Wilde on screen), 90 (gay stereotypes), 91 (defining camp), 92 ('sissies'), 93 ('tomboys'), 94 (the prison genre), 100 (gays as villains), 102 (Dirk Bogarde), 103 (lesbian vampires), 104 (Montgomery Clift), 110 (gays in horror films), 111 (Carmen Miranda), 117 ('buddy movies'), 124 (parents of gays in films), 129/130 (pornography), 146 (Eisenstein), 158 (gays and race in films), 181 (Hitchcock), 183 (schoolgirls), 184 (schoolboys), etc.

Becker, Raymond de, 'Notes sur un cinéma homophile', *Arcadie*, 74, Feb 60, pp. 97–100.

Britton, Andrew, 'Sexuality and Power', *Framework*, no. 6; 'For Interpretation, Against Camp', *Gay Left*, Winter 78/79.

Dyer, Richard, 'Gays in films', *Gay Left* no. 2; 'Pasolini and Homosexuality' in Paul Willemen (ed.), *Pier Paolo Pasolini*, British Film Institute, 1976; 'Homosexuality and Film Noir', *Jump Cut*, no. 16; 'It's being so camp as keeps us going', *Body Politic*, no. 36, Sept 77; '*Victim:* Hegemonic Project', *Film Form* no. 2; 'Reading Fassbinder's Sexual Politics' in Tony Rayns (ed.), *Fassbinder* (revised edition), British Film Institute, 1980.

Hennigan, Alison, 'In Camera' (on Jacqueline Audry), *Gay News*, no. 168.

Howard, Rolland, 'Homosexuality as a vehicle for masochism symbolised in the film *Fireworks*', *Mattachine Review*, 7 (7), July 61, pp. 6–8.

Jester, Klaus, 'Den "Normalen" ihre eigene Betroffenheit bewusst machen', *Cinéma* (Switzerland), no. 3, 77, pp. 20–32.

Martin, Donna, 'Lesbianism in the Movies', *GPU News* (Wisconsin), Aug 75, reprinted *Gay News*, no. 82.

Mellen, Joan, 'Lesbianism in the Movies', in *Women and their Sexuality in the New Film*, Davis-Poynter, London, 1974.

Meyers, Janet, 'Dyke goes to the Movies', *Dyke* (New York), Spring 76.

Olson, Ray, 'Affecting but too Evasive: Gay Film Work', *Jump Cut*, no. 20.

Pearce, Frank, 'How to be immoral and ill, pathetic and dangerous, all at the same time: mass media and homosexuality', in Stanley Cohen and Jock Young (eds.), *The Manufacture of News*, Constable, London, 1973, pp. 284–301.

Peck, Ron and Hallam, Paul, 'Images of Homosexuality' *Gay Left*, no. 5.

Phillips, Gene D., 'The Boys on the Bandwagon; Homosexuality in the Movies', in Thomas R. Atkins (ed.) *Sexuality in the Movies*, Indiana University Press, 1975, pp. 157–171.

Purdon, Noel, 'Gay Cinema', *Cinema Papers* (Melbourne), no. 10, Sept–Oct 76.

Russo, Vito, 'The closet syndrome: Gays in Hollywood', *Village Voice*, June 25, 1979; *The Celluloid Closet* (forthcoming).

Scheugl, Hans, *Sexualität und Nevrose im Film*, Mauser, Munich, 1974.

Siebenand, Paul Alcuin, *The Beginnings of Gay Cinema in Los Angeles: the industry and the audience*, doctoral dissertation, University of California (Department of Communications), 1975.

Stimpson, Mansel, 'Gaily Gaily', *Montage*, no. 42, 1978, pp. 12–14.

Turan, Kenneth and Zite, Stephen F., *Sinema: American Pornographic Films and the People Who Make Them*, Praeger, New York, 1974.

Tyler, Parker, *Screening the Sexes*, Holt, Rinehart and Winston, New York, 1972.

Vogel, Amos, 'The breaking of sexual taboos; homosexuality and other variants', in *Film as a Subversive Art*, Wiedenfeld and Nicolson, London, 1975.

Wilson, Elizabeth, 'How much is it worth?', *Red Rag*, no. 10, pp. 6–9 (on *The Bitter Tears of Petra von Kant* and *A Bigger Splash*).

Waugh, Tom, 'Rainer Werner Fassbinder', *Body Politic*, no. 29; 'A fag-spotter's guide to Eisenstein', *Body Politic*, July–Aug 1977; 'Films by Gays for Gays',*Jump Cut*, no. 16.

Wood, Robin, 'Responsibilities of a Gay Film Critic', *Film Comment*, Jan–Feb 1978.

SUPPLEMENT TO FILMOGRAPHY

INTRODUCTION

When is a representation of a gay person not a representation of a gay person?

(i) When the character is a lesbian who confounds definition by finding 'true' sexual fulfilment with a man. This scenario accounts for most heterosexual-orientated pornographic films. I stand by Richard Dyer's argument for including pornographic films (p. 2), and claim with others that there are specific, important differences between those designed for straight (male) audiences and those produced for gay (male) audiences. The American Film Institute Catalogue lists hundreds of films of both types which, made in the 1960s, are of historical significance. Mentioned here are only those that truly invoke new-found sexual freedom by explicitly involving gay themes or central characters. Among these are many intelligent and subversive dramas–do not be deceived by their drearily heterosexist titles. Also included in this supplement are a large number of 1970s gay male porn films–from a decade when thorough documentation of such becomes extremely difficult–where there is a reference available for further information.

(ii) When the character goes no further than refusing to comply with the heterosexual expectations. This is something common to recent films as diverse as Alan Moyle's *Times Square* and Rachel Finkelstein's *Three Short Episodes*. Protagonists in these films actively refuse heterosexual relations and demands–yet it is surely as oppressive as the sexism these characters reject to call their positions gay. The films may be lesbian in the way that Caroline Sheldon describes, or they may strongly appeal to a gay sensibility (p. 40), but only where the dominant reading is one that sees gay characters or relationships on the screen are they mentioned in this catalogue.

(iii) When the characters appear in experimental or 'non-professional' films. Here, the need for stereotyping and easy identification is not as necessary as in mainstream cinema (p. 32). At the same time, in the work of avant-gardists like Gregory Markopoulos gay characters are used to signal the film's sideways 'departure' from cinematic norms. Many contemporary experimental film-makers want to abandon completely traditional notions of actors playing roles. Similarly, the increased accessibility of Super-8 film and domestic video equipment means that more 'home movies' are being produced; in these, gay women and men may appear to play themselves, sometimes treating gayness as a vital but unspoken given. These non-professional documents complement the work of people like Jeanette Iljon and Bruno de Florence in their questioning of representation. Our definition of what constitutes a gay representation has shifted accordingly, to take notice of these films.

The three areas outlined above are not the only ones which perplex the compiler of a gay filmography. Others, like these, engage issues of the screening context and film availability. *Celine et Julie vont en bateau* is easily perceived as a representation of a lesbian relationship when programmed next to *The Killing of Sister George* or Jacqui Deuckworth's *Home-Made Melodrama*. In this way, the intentions of the film-makers blur with the expectations of an audience. From the potential multiple results of this encounter, I have tried to consider the most frequent context of the film 'event' and the various historical and cultural factors surrounding its making. For the first time, material made for television is also included in this filmography: programmes currently available for rental on film, and tv movies. It seems to me that, as well as a grasp of the variations in the screening context, some idea of availability and accessibility must be fed into the writing of a gay filmography. Whilst the inclusion of Mauritz Stiller's *Vingarne* is exciting as an example of very early gay portrayal, it is, in truth—since no copies of *Vingarne* survive—through films like *A Question of Love* that most people will explore the devices of representation.

M.F.

Abnormal Female, The; USA, 1969; (Raders); Pamela Berkeley, Jeanette Foster; *AFIC* F6, p. 1
Abuse; USA, 1982; (Bressan); Richard Ryder, Raphael Sbarge; *Variety* 23.3.83, p. 24
abysses, Les; Fr, 1963; (Papatkis); Francine Bergé, Colette Bergé; *AFIC* F6, p. 1
AC/DC; USA, 1969; (Winters); Gale Forester, Judy Sacks; *AFIC* F6, p. 2
Aceto; It, 1977 8mm; (De Generate); *CinémAction* no. 15 1981, p. 162
Achter Glass (Behind the Glass, a Love Story Among Other Things); Neths, 1980 mtv; (Ieperen); Elias van Zanden, Rudolf Lucieer
Adam's Rib; USA, 1949; (Cukor); David Wayne; *MFB* 17, p. 22
Adversary, The; USA, 1970; (Klein); Howard Lawrence; *Variety* 1.4.70, p. 24
After the Game; Austr, 1977; (Gray); *GN* 191, p. 13
Age of Consent; USA, 198-video
Al Castello; It, 1980; (Renda)
Alexander: The Other Side of Dawn; USA, 1976 mtv; (Erman); Leigh J. McCloskey; *Hollywood Reporter* 16.5.77, p. 4
Alice in Acidland; USA, 1969; (Donne); *AFIC* F6, p. 16
Alla Piu 'Bella; It, 1977; (Melano); *CinémAction* no. 15 1981, pp. 137-140
All Night Rider; USA, 1969; (Findlay); *AFIC* F6, p. 19
All the Way Down; USA, 1968; (Spencer); *AFIC* F6, p. 20
All Together Now; USA, 1970; (Allan); Cileste Eslar, Ela Mitzo; *AFIC* F6, p. 21
Altered Habits; 1981; (Newman)
Always on Sundays (see *Tales for Males*)
Amarsi Male; It, 1969; (di Leo); Susan Scott; *Cinema d'Oggi* 25.8.69, p. 33
Amazones d'hier, lesbiennes d'aujourd'hui; Can, 1981 video; (Brunet/Charest/Turcotte-/Bergeron)
Amen; Belg, 1975; (Mahauden); Roland Mahauden, Olivier de Saedeleer
American Gigolo; USA, 1980; (Schrader); Richard Gere, Nina van Pallandt; *MFB* 47, p. 87
AMG Story, The; USA; (Mizer); Siebenand, p. 49
Am I Female?; USA, 1970; Warren St. Thomas, Jennifer Kelly; *AFIC* F6, p. 21
amis, Les; Fr, 1971; (Blain); Yann Favre-Epstein, Philippe March; *Variety* 9.6.71, p. 17
Anatomy of Tom; USA, 1969?; (Rocco); Siebenand, p. 58
And Five Makes Jason; USA, 1969; (Stagg); Kathy Harriet; *AFIC* F6, p. 28
And Give Us Our Daily Sex (see *Malizia erotica*)
Andy Warhol and His Clan; Ger, 1970; (Koetter); Joe D'Allesandro, Taylor Mead; *MFB* 38, p. 135
Angel, Angel, Down We Go; USA, 1969; (Thom); Jordan Christopher, Charles Aidman; *AFIC* F6, p. 30
Angelique in Black Leather; USA, 1968; (Bouchet); Angelique Bouchet, Maria Lennard; *AFIC* F6, p. 32
Angelos; Gr, 1982; (Katacuzenos); *GN* 263, p. 3
Angle; Fr, 1976 S8; (Nedjar); *CinémAction* no. 15 1981, p. 161
Anna und Edith; Ger, 1975; (Neuhaus)
An Old Refrain; GB, 1983 S8; (Beven)
Another Country; GB, 1983; (Kanievska); Cary Elwes; *Screen International* no. 406 6-13.8.83, p. 14

Another Way (see *Egymásra nézve*)
Apartment; Austr, 1977; (McMurchy)
Aphrodisiacs and the Male Animal; USA, 1970; (DeSimone); Siebenand, p. 108
Apocalypse - K - Distranjo; Curacao? S8; (Le Rooy)
Apparence féminine; Fr, 1979; (Rein); Dominique D.; *Altro Cinema* no. 30-31, p. 34
Arabian Boy in Paris; Fr, 1979; (Archenoul)
aspect rose de la chose, L'; Fr, 1980; (Wong); *CinémAction* no. 15 1981, pp. 97-98
Assault; USA, 1970; (DeSimone); Siebenand, p. 108
Atami Blues; USA, 1962; (Richie)
A tout prendre; Can, 1963; (Jutra); Claude Jutra; *Variety* 28.8.63, p. 18/*Copie Zero* no. 11 1981, p. 23
Attitude Triptych - The Setting; GB, 1982 S8; (Allen); Gilles Sherwell
Aus dem Leben der Marionetten (From the Life of the Marionettes); Ger, 1980; (Bergman); Walter Schmidinger; *MFB* 48, p. 88
Autumn Nocturne; USA, 1969; (Rocco); Siebenand, p. 58
Available Space; USA, 1978; (Hammer); *Film Reader* no. 5 1982, pp. 60-66

Bad Boys; USA, 1983; (Rosenthal); Clancy Brown, Robert Lee Rush; *MFB* 50, p. 128
Balcony, The; USA, 1963; (Strick); Shelley Winters, Lee Grant; *MFB* 30, p. 167
Balling Wonder Bread; USA, 198-video; (Simon)
Bang Bang Gang, The; USA, 1970; (Guylder); Bambi Allen; *AFIC* F6, p. 62
banque du sperme, La ; Fr, 1974; (Chabal/Genet)
Basel Quartet, The (see *Il Quartetto Basileus*)
Bauer von Babylon (Wizard of Babylon); Ger, 1982; (Schidor); Rainer Werner Fassbinder; *Variety* 1.9.82, p. 9
Beastly Treatment; GB, 1979; (Foulk); Joe Figg
Beat; Can, 1976; (Blanchard); Bertrand Gagnon; *New Canadian Film* no. 38-39 vol. 8 1977, p. 13
Behind the Glass, a Love Story Among Other Things (see *Achter Glass*)
Belle, La; Gr; (Spetsiotis); *CinémAction* no. 15 1981, p. 162
Bell Jar, The; USA, 1979; (Peerce); Donna Mitchell; *Variety* 21.3.79
Beneath the Valley of the Ultravixens (Ultravixens); USA, 1979; (Meyer); Ken Kerr
Berlin Blues (see *Stadt der verlorenen Seelen*)
Berliner Bettwurst; Ger, 1977; (Praunheim); Deitmar Kracht; *Variety* 16.2.77, p. 26
Berlin-Harlem; Ger, 1974; (Lambert); Conrad Jennings; *Filmecho/Filmwoche* no. 62 7.11.75, p. 10
Best Man, The; USA, 1964; (Wheeler); Cliff Robertson; *AFIC* F6, p. 80
Betörung der blauen Matrosen, Die; Ger, 1975; Valeska Gert, Rosa von Praunheim
Bette Davis' Last Try; It, 1976; (Farri); Edmondo Roth
Betty Walters Interview Show; USA, 1981 video; (Brune); Paul Brune
Between Men; USA, 1978; (Roberts)
Big Bares; USA, 1968; (Rocco); Siebenand, p. 58
Big Muscle; USA, 1969; (Rocco); Siebenand, p. 58
Big Sleep, The; USA, 1946; (Hawks); Tom Rafferty, Theodore von Eltz; *MFB* 45, p. 185
Bilder-Video bei uns zuhaus; Ger, 1981; (Speck)
Bionda Fragola (Strawberry Blonde); It, 1980; (Bellei); Mino Bellei, Umberto Orsim; *Altro Cinema* no. 30-31 1981, p. 8
Black and Blue; USA, 1971; (DeSimone); Siebenand, p. 108
Blonde Cobra; USA, 1959-63; (Jacobs); Jack Smith, Jerry Sims; *MFB* 50, p. 226
Blood Money; USA, 1933; (Brown); Sandra Shaw; Russo, p. 44
Blood-Spattered Bride, The (see *La Novia ensangrentada*)
Blue Movie Audition; USA, 1974; (DeSimone); Siebenand, p. 108
Blue Prelude; USA, 1969?; (Rocco); Siebenand, p. 58
Blue Streak; USA, 1971; (Rappaport)
Blue Summer Breeze, A; USA, 1972; (Knight); Siebenand, p. 124

Blusburts; Fr, S8; (Pilot); *CinémAction* no. 15 1981, p. 161
Born in Flames; USA, 1983; (Borden); Honey, Adele Bertei
Boy and His Dog, A; USA, 1969?; (Rocco); Siebenand, p. 58
Boy Friend 1; Fr, 1977 S8; (Soukaz); *CinémAction* no. 15 1981, p. 161
Boy into Man; USA, 1970; (Eden); *AFIC* F6, p. 117
Boynapped; USA, 197-; (Logan); *GN* 175
Boy Play; USA, 1969; (Rocco); Siebenand, p. 58
Boys in Chains; USA, 1969; *AFIC* F6, p. 119
Boys in the Woods; USA, 1969; (Rocco); Siebenand, p. 58
Boys on the Run; USA, 1969; (Rocco); Siebenand, p. 58
Boy, the Wood, and the Body, The; USA, 1968; (Rocco); Siebenand, p. 58
Boxing Match; Fr, 1974 S8; (Mendelson); *CinémAction* no. 15 1981, p. 161
Brand of Shame; USA, 1968; (Elliott); Vanessa Van Dyke; *AFIC* F6, p. 121
Bread'n'Gravy; GB, 1982 S8; (Bell)
Brick Dollhouse, The; USA, 1967; (Martinez); Frankie O'Brien; *AFIC* F6, p. 124
Bride for Brenda, A; USA, 1969; (Goetz); Lois Lane, Rita Joyce; *AFIC* F6, p. 124
Brothel; USA, 1966; (Vehr); Jack Smith, Mario Montez; *AFIC* F6, p. 127
Brothers; USA; (Elliott/Sato); Siebenand, p. 126
Bruised Angel; USA, 197-; (Figg); *GN* 175
Bushido; Jap, 1963; (Imai); Kinnosuke Nakamura, Yoshika Mita; *Variety* 3.7.63, p. 6
Bushwhacker, The; USA, 1968; (Elliott); Acee Decee; *AFIC* F6, p. 135
By Design; Can, 1981; (Jutra); Patty Duke Astin, Sara Botsford; *Variety* 3.6.81, p. 23

cage aux folles II, La; Fr, 1980; (Molinaro); Ugo Tognazzi, Michel Serrault; *MFB* 48, p. 89
Caged Desires; USA, 1970; (Davis); Barbara Peeters; *AFIC* F6, p. 138
Caged Heat; USA, 1974; (Demme); Juanita Brown, Roberta Collins; *MFB* 42, p. 258
California Suite; USA, 1978; (Ross); Michael Caine; *MFB* 46, p. 69
Caligula; USA/It, 1979; (Brass/Guccione); Teresa Ann Savoy, Helen Mirren; *MFB* 47, p. 232
Call Her Savage; USA, 1932; (Dillon); Clara Bow; Russo, pp. 42-43
Cambio de Sexo (I Want to Be a Woman); Sp. 1977; (Aranda); Victoria Abril; *MFB* 48, p. 63
Camera en quete; Fr, 1975 S8; (Roncier/Gros); *CinémAction* no. 15 1981, p. 161
Can't Stop the Music; USA, 1980; (Walker); The Village People; *MFB* 47, p. 153
Ca peut pas être l'hiver, on n'a même pas eu d'été; Can, 1980; (Carre); Serge Belair; *Variety* 22.4.81, p. 26
Carmen; Ger, 1977 S8; (Bockmayer); *CinémAction* no. 15 1981, p. 160
Carrousel; USA, 198-video; (Baker?)
Car Wash; USA, 1976; (Schultz); Antonio Fargas; *MFB* 44, p. 19
Caso di Coscienza, Un; It, 1969; (Grimaldi); Antonella Lualdi, Francoise Prévost; *Intermezzo* no. 9-10 31.5.70, p. 4
Casta Diva; Neths, 1982; (de Kuyper); Jack Post, Emil Poppe
Casual Relations; USA, 1973; (Rappaport); Sis Smith, Mel Austin; *Cinefantastique* Autumn 1974, p. 35
Catch Me When I Fall; USA, 1970; *AFIC* F6, p. 158
Catch 69; USA, 1970; *AFIC* F6, p. 158
Cats, The; Swed, 1969; (Carlsen); Eva Dahlbeck, Gio Petré; *AFIC* F6, p. 161
Caught; USA, 1948; (Ophuls); Curt Bois; *MFB* 16, p. 82
Celine et Julie vont en bateau (Celine and Julie Go Boating); Fr, 1974; (Rivette); Juliet Berto, Dominique Labourier; *MFB* 43, p. 163
Ce même corps qui m'attire; Fr, 1981; (Labrune)
Certain Desire, A; GB, 1980; (de Florence); Mary Evans, Stephen Gee; *GN* 196, p. 27
Chained; USA, 1973; (DeSimone); Siebenand, p. 109
Chained Girls; USA, 1965; (Weiss); *AFIC* F6, p. 161
Challenge, The; USA, 1968; (Rocco); Siebenand, p. 58

chambre des phantasmes, La; Fr, 1979; (Sénécal); *Altro Cinema* no. 30-31, p. 34
Changes; GB, 197-; (Duckworth)
chats bottés, Les; Can, 1971; (Fournier); *Film Canadiana* vol. 3 no. 1 1972, p. 16
chica de las bragas transparentes, La (*Pick-Up Girls*); Sp, 1980; (Franco); Rosa Velenty; *MFB* 50, p. 185
chiens chauds, Les; Can, 1980; (Fournier); Harry Reems; *Cinema Canada* no. 69 1980, pp. 29-30
Chinese Checkers; USA/GB, 1965; (Dwoskin); Beverley Grant, Joan Alder; *BNFC* June 1969
Christiane F. wir Kinder vom Bahnhof Zoo (*Christiane F.*); Ger, 1981; (Edel); Thomas Haustein; *MFB* 47, p. 5
Chu Hai Tang; Jap/Ch, 1943; Russo, p. 249
Cinema Work; GB; (Moule/Morris)
Circle Line; Fr; (Suerta)
cite des neuf portes, La; Fr, 1977 S8; (Marti); *CinémAction* no. 15 1981, p. 161
City of Lost Souls (see *Stadt der verlorenen Seelen*)
Claire et l'obscur (*Claire and Darkness*); Switz, 1982; (Haralambis); Achille Tzonis, Dwight Rodrick; *Variety* 25.8.82, p. 15
Claude et Greta (*Her and She and Him*); Fr, 1970; (Pecas); Astrid Frank, Nicole Debonne; *AFIC* F6, p. 472
Clinic, The; Austr, 1982; (Stevens); Chris Haywood; *MFB* 50, p. 129
Club de femmes; Fr, 1936; (Deval); Danielle Darrieux; *Catalogue des film francais 1929-39* ref. 280
Collection, The; USA, 1970; (DeSimone); Max Blue, David Michaels
Come Back to the 5 & Dime Jimmy Dean, Jimmy Dean; USA, 1982; (Altman); Karen Black, Mark Patton; *MFB* 50, p. 231
Come to the Orgy; USA, 197-; (Brian); *GN* 175
Coming Out; GB, 1975 mtv; (Carr); *BNFC* vol. 14 1976
Coming Out; GB, 1979 mtv; (Wiseman); Lewis Duncan, Nigel Havers; *Radio Times* 28.4-4.5.79, p. 102
Coming Out; USA, 197-; (Berkeley Lesbian Feminist Film Collective)
Coming to Know; USA, 1976; (Ashton)
Comme une femme; Fr, 1979; (Dura); Pascale, Patrick Guillemin; *Altro Cinema* no. 30-31, p. 32
confesse, La (*Interdits*); Fr, 1978; (Rémy)
Confessions of Lady Blue; USA, 1978; (Fabritzi); Maureen Spring, Gloria Leonard; *MFB* 49, p. 197
Contes Pervers (*Erotic Tales*); Fr/It, 1980; (Deforges); Carina Barone, Béatrice; *MFB* 49, p. 290
Conundrum Clinique; Can, 1981 video; (Campbell)
Cool Hands, Warm Heart; USA, 1979; (Friedrich)
Corner of the Circle; USA, 1975; (Daughton); Michael Nobel, Nick Plakias; *Cahiers du cinéma* no. 273, pp. 57-58
Cosi' Dolce Cosi' Perversa; It, 1969; (Lenzi); Carroll Baker, Erika Blanc; *Cinema d'Oggi* 15.12.69, p. 10
Couples and Robbers; GB, 1981; (Peploe); Peter Eyre, Frank Grimes; *MFB* 49, p. 214
Craig; USA, 1970; Scot Arden; *AFIC* F6, p. 210
Cristo; Fr, 1977 S8; (Hernandez); *CinémAction* no. 15 1981, p. 161
Crushed Lilies; USA, 1982 video; (Jankowski?)
Cucarecord; Sp, 1978 S8; (5 QK collective); *CinémAction* no. 15 1981, p. 161

Dad and Dave Come to Town (*The Rudd Family Goes to Town*); Austr, 1938; (Hall); Alec Kellaway; *MFB* 6, p. 42
Dance of the Sex Orgy; USA, 1969; (Rocco); Siebenand, p. 58
Dark Side of Tomorrow, The; USA, 1970; (Novik); Elizabeth Plumb, Alisa Courtney; *AFIC* F6, p. 228

David, Montgomery and I; USA, 1979; (Speck)
Dear Boys (see *Lieve Jongens*)
Death and Transfiguration; GB, 1983; (Davies); Wilfred Brambell
Deathtrap; USA, 1982; (Lumet); Michael Caine, Christopher Reeve; *MFB* 49, p. 197
Deathwatch; USA, 1966; (Morrow); Leonard Nimoy, Paul Mazursky; *AFIC* F6, p. 243
Deep in Silent Dialogue; Ger, 1980; (Aurand)
Delivrez-nous du mal; Can, 1965; (Lord); Yvon Deschamps; *Copie Zero* no. 11 1981, pp. 16-17
Demi-Gods; Fr; (Potts); *CinémAction* no. 15 1981, p. 161
Depart to Arrive; Ger, 1982; (von Grote); Gabriele Ossburg, Ute Cremer; *Variety* 21.4.82, p. 18
dernier métro, Le (*The Last Metro*); Fr, 1980; (Truffaut); Andréa Ferréol; *MFB* 48, p. 135
Desbrosses; USA; (Fitz); *CinémAction* no. 15 1981, p. 163
Desert of the Heart; USA, 1982?; (Deitch); *Advocate* no. 341 29.4.82, pp. 45-46
Desire; Austr., 1980; (Ingram); Michael Hannon, Michael Lore
Désiré; Can, 1981; (Langlois); Josee Labossiere, Johane Seymour; *Cinema Canada* no. 85 1982, p. 28
Detention Girls; USA, 1969; *AFIC* F6, p. 250
Deux lions au soleil (*Two Lions in the Sun*); Fr, 1980; (Feraldo); Jean-Francois Stevenin, Jean-Pierre Sentier; *Variety* 3.9.80, pp. 25-26
Devastated City; GB, 1980
Devil's Playground, The; Austr, 1976; (Schepsi); Arthur Dignam, Michael David; *MFB* 44, p. 167
Dichotomy; USA, 197-; (Goldam); *Jump Cut* no. 20 1980, p. 10
Die Lady (*Games of Desire*); Fr/Ger, 1966; (Albin/ Berneis); Paul Hubschmid; *AFIC* F6, p. 388
Dirnenschicksal; Ger, 1980; (Eichhorn); Christoph Eichhorn, Wieland Speck
Dirty Daughters (see *Die Hure und der Hurensohn*)
Discobolos (see *Tales for Males*)
Disneyland Discovery; USA, 1968; (Rocco); Siebenand, p. 58
Divided Loyalties; USA; (Sonbent); *CinémAction* no. 15 1981, p. 154
Donna del Domenica, La; It, 1975; (Commencini)
Don't Push Me; USA, 1970; Brian Reynolds; *AFIC* F6, p. 280
Dossier 51; Fr/Ger, 1978; (Deville); Francois Marthouret; *Variety* 31.5.78, p. 28
Double Exposure; USA, 1968; (Rocco); Siebenand, p. 58
Double Initiation; USA, 1970; (Tobalina); Janet Wass, Jeannie Anderson; *AFIC* F6, p. 282
Double Labyrinthe; Fr, 1976 S8; (Klonaris/Tomadaki); *CinémAction* no. 15 1981, p. 161
Double Strength; USA, 1978; (Hammer); Barbara Hammer, Terry Sendgraff; *Jump Cut* no. 24-25 1981, p. 29
Dozens, The; USA, 1980; (Dall/Conrad); Debra Margolies; *GN* 205, p. iv
Dragues; Fr, 1978; (Terry); Tony Weber, Bertrand Licart; *Ecran* no. 73 1978, p. 75
Dream A40; GB, 1965; (Reckord); Michael Billington, Nicholas Wright; *MFB* 38, p. 172
Dream Age; USA, 1979; (Hammer); *Film Reader* no. 5 1982, pp. 63-65
Dream Life (see *La vie rêvée*)
Drifter (*Two Way Drift*); USA, 197-; (Rocco); Joe Adair, David Russell; *Variety* 24.9.79, p. 24
Drifting; 1983; (Guttman); Jonathan Segal; *Variety* 17.8.83, p. 41
Duets; USA; (Sherwood); *CinémAction* no. 15 1981, p. 163
Duffy's Tavern; USA, 1970; (DeSimone); Siebenand, p. 108
Dusk Glow; USA, 1969?; (Rocco); Siebenand, p. 58
Dust unto Dust; USA; (DeSimone); Siebenand, pp. 87, 108

Early to Bed; USA, 1968; (Rocco); Siebenand, p. 58
Ecstasy Girls; USA, 1970; (Janovich); Serena, Rita Allen, Sheri Laky; *MFB* 48, p. 91
Egymásra nézve (*Another Way*); Hung, 1982; (Makk); Jadwiga Jankowska-Cieslak, Grażyna Szapolowska; *MFB* 49, p. 262

ll x 14; USA, 1977; (Benning); Serafina Bathrick, Paddy Whannel; *MFB* 45, p. 6
Ella, une vraie famille; Fr, 1980; (Gorki); *CinémAction* no. 15 1981, p. 136
Elle, Marcel; Fr, 1973 S8; (Marx); *CinémAction* no. 15 1981, p. 161
Emma la banquierre; Fr, 198-; (Girod); Romy Schneider, Marie-France Pisier
End, The; USA, 1969?; (Rocco); Siebenand, p. 58
End as a Man (The Strange One); USA, 1957; (Garfein); Ben Gazzara, Paul Richards; *MFB* 24, p. 96
Ende des Regenbogens, Das (End of the Rainbow); Ger, 1979 mtv; (Friessner); Thomas Kufahl; *Variety* 31.10.79, p. 42
Equation a deux inconnus; Fr, 1980; (de Velsa); *Altro Cinema* no. 30-31 1981, p. 33
Erikas Leidenschaften (Erika's Passions); Ger, 1976; (Stöckl); Karin Baal, Vera Tschechowa; *Variety* 8.11.78, p. 18
Eros, 0 Basileus; USA, 1967; (Markopoulos); *AFIC* F6, p. 306
Erotic Tales (see *Contes Pervers*)
Erotikus - A History of the Gay Movies; USA, 1972; (DeSimone); *Variety* 8.8.73, p. 14
Everything Goes; USA, 1974; (DeSimone); Siebenand, p. 109
Evil Under the Sun; GB, 1981; (Hamilton); Roddy McDowall; *MFB* 49, p. 83
Exclusive Sailor, The; Fr, 1923-25; *Body Politic* no. 90 1983, p. 30
Execution, The (see *Martin*)
Exil; Fr; (Landy); Francoise le Taëron
Exotica Numero Una; USA; (Holloway/Still)
Ex und Hopp; Ger, 1976; (Lambert); Lothar Lambert, Wolfgang Breiter; *Variety* 16.3.77, p. 24

Face à Face; Fr; (Rock)
Fame; USA, 1980; (Parker); Paul McCrane; *MFB* 47, p. 130
Fanny's Hill; USA, 1968; (Rocco); Siebenand, p. 58
Fantastica; Can/Fr, 1980; (Carle); Carol Laure; *Variety* 14.5.80, p. 14
Farewell to Charms, A; Austr, 1979; (Sklan?); Radda Jordan, Helen Pankhurst, Stretch
Fat Black Pussycat, The; USA, 1964; (Lea); *AFIC* F6, p. 328
Felicia; USA, 1969; (Shiffen); Jo Ellen; *AFIC* F6, p. 332
Femme d'à côté, La (The Woman Next Door); Fr, 1981; (Truffaut); Roger Van Hool; *MFB* 49, p. 27
Fesses en feu; Fr, 1978; (Koenigwerter); Jean-Sebastien Davy, Emmanuel dos Santos; *Altro Cinema* no. 30-31 1981, p. 34
Fight, The; video; (Orvino)
Filma, Una; It, 1977 S8; (FFAG); *CinémAction* no.15 1981, p. 163
Film for Two; (Mignatti)
Filmworks (see *Gay Is Out*)
Five Minutes, Miss Lenska; USA?; (Gaspar); *GN* 191, p. 13
Flikkerij; Neths, 1975 S8; (de Vries); *CinémAction* no. 15 1981, p. 162
Flesh Hustler, The; USA, 1970; (Irving); Mark Royal; *AFIC* F6, p. 355
Flesh on Glass; Austr, 1980; (Turner)
Flikkerij 2; Neths, 1976 S8; (Nagtigaal); *CinémAction* no. 15 1981, p. 162
Flower Thief, The; USA, 1962; (Rice); Taylor Mead; *AFIC* F6, p. 358
Focii; GB, 1975; (Iljon); Jeanette Iljon; *BNFC* vol. 17 1979, p. 152
Fooling of the Blue Sailor, The (see *Die Betörung der blauen Matrosen*)
Forbidden Letters; USA, 1978; (Bressan); Robert Adams, Richard Locke
Forty Deuce; USA, 1981; (Morrisey)
Fouras Feeling; Fr, 1976 S8; (Landy); *CinémAction* no. 15 1981, p. 161
491; Swed, 1963; (Sjöman); Frank Sundstrom; *Variety* 22.1.64, p. 19
Fourth Man, The (see *De Vierde Man*)
Fuori Uno; It, 1973 S8; (*Fouri* Collective); *CinémAction* no. 15 1981, p. 163
Framed Youth - Revenge of the Teenage Perverts; GB, 1983 video; (Lesbian & Gay Youth Video Project); *MFB* 50, p. 255
Fraternity, The; USA, 1970; *AFIC* F6, p. 374

Free Soul (see *Let There Be Boys*)
Freia und Ferry; Ger, 1980; (Eichhorn); Christoph Eichhorn
French Film; Fr, 1983 S8; (Bell)
Friday Night Adventure (Vitale)
From the Life of the Marionettes (see *Aus dem Leben der Marionetten*)
Fucking City (see *Verdammte Stadt*)
Fuga di Casa; It, 1973 S8; (Amidiei); *CinémAction* no. 15 1981

Galaxy; USA, 1966; (Markopoulos); Allen Ginsberg, Peter Orlovsky; *Chicago Daily News* 17.12.66
Games Men Play; USA, 197-; (Janson); Jayson McBride
Games of Desire (see *Die Lady*)
Games Without Rules; USA, 1970; (DeSimone); Siebenand, p. 108
Gang Bang; USA, 1970; AFIC F6, p. 388
garcon comme toi et moi, Un; Fr, 1979; (Fabrizzi); Francois Chaument, Yannick Sartof; *Altro Cinema* no. 30-31 1981, p. 32
Gay Divorcee, The; USA, 1934; (Sandrich); Edward Everett Horton; Russo, pp. 35-36
Gay Guide to Cheating; USA, 1970; (DeSimone); Siebenand, p. 108
Gay Guide to Hawaii; USA, 1970; (DeSimone); Siebenand, p. 108
Gay Guide to the Campus; USA, 1970; (DeSimone); Siebenand, p. 108
Gay Is Out (*Filmworks*); USA, 1980; (Manfredini)
Gay New Male, A; USA; (Sutto); *CinémAction* no. 15 1981, p. 163
Gay Power - Gay Politics; USA, 1980 mtv; (Diekhaus/Crile)
Gay Voices; GB, 197-; (Britton/Jeffery)
Gender; USA; (Calderwood)
Gently Down the Stream; USA, 1981; (Friedrich)
Georgia, Georgia; Swed, 1971; (Bjorkman); Roger Furman; *Films in Sweden* no. 2 1972, pp. 51-54
Gerausch rasche Erlösung, Das (*The Sound of Fast Relief*); Ger, 1982; (Speck)
Getting Ready; USA; (Meyers)
Ghetto Girls; USA, 1980 video; (Canaly/Monroe); Sheri Pittman, Vivian Beauty
Ghost of a Chance; USA, 1973; (Hall); Jimmy Hughes
Gigolo My Love; Fr, 1978; (Archenoul); *La revue du cinéma* no. 353 1980, p. 98
Gilles, Jose, Marcel; Fr, 1976; (Kut); *CinémAction* no. 15 1981, p. 161
Girlfriends; USA, 1978; (Weill); Amy Wright; *MFB* 45, p. 175
Girl from Pussy Cat, The; USA, 1969; AFIC F6, p. 400
Girl with Hungry Eyes, The; USA, 1966; (Rotsler); Cathey Crowfoot; AFIC F6, p. 405
Giselle; Braz, 1975; (DiMello); Alba Valeria, Monique LaFond; *Variety* 6.10.82, p. 14
Greek Gods; USA, 1954; Artie Zeller, Bob del Montegue, Jimmy Apolo; *Body Politic* no. 90 1983, p. 32
Greengage Summer, The (see *Loss of Innocence*)
Greetings from Washington DC; USA, 1981; (Winer)
Greta's Girls; USA; (Schiller/Said)
Groovy Guy 1969; USA, 1969; (Rocco); Siebenand, p. 58 (see also *Mondo Rocco*)
Groovy Guy 1970; USA, 1970?; (Rocco); Siebenand, p. 58
Groovy Guy 1971?; USA, 1971; (Rocco); Jimmy Hughes; Siebenand, p. 58
Groovy Guy 1972; USA, 1972?; (Rocco); Siebenand, p. 58
Growing Up: Brad; Austr, 1977; (Noyce); *BNFC* 1982, p. 48
Growing Up: Jenny; Austr, 1977; (Sharp); *BNFC* 1982, p. 48
Gypsy's Ball, The; USA, 1970; (DeSimone); Siebenand, p. 108
Hair Revisited; USA, 1970?; (Rocco); Siebenand, p. 58 (see also *Mondo Rocco*)
Hang Loose; USA, 1970; AFIC F6, p. 450
Happy Birthday, Davy (see *I Am Curious Gay*)
Happy Birthday Gemini; Can, 1980; (Benner); Allen Rosenberg; *MFB* 48, p. 17
Hatsukoi jigokuhen (*Nanami: Inferno of First Love*); Jap, 1968; Akio Takahashi, Kuniko Ishii; AFIC F6, p. 756

Head Lady; USA, 1968; (Elliott); Bermuda Schwartz, Vanessa Van Dyke; *AFIC* F6, p. 472

Heat Wave; USA, 1964; Jim Fanning, Luis Speedy Gonzalez; *Body Politic* no. 90 1983, p. 33

Her and She and Him (see *Claude et Greta*)

Here and Now; GB, 1983 mtv

Hermes Bird; 1981; (Broughton)

Hey, Look Me Over; USA, 1969; (Rocco); Siebenand, p. 58

Hide and Seek (see *Miskhak Makhbuim*)

histoire des femmes, Une; Can, 1980; (Rock)

hiver approche, L'; Fr, 1974; (Bensoussan); Catherine Lachens, Michele Vernard

hiver bleu, L'; Can, 198-; (Blanchard); *Cinema Canada* no. 80 Dec 1981-Jan 1982, pp. 28-30

Hombre Llamado Flor de Otonō, Un (*A Man Called Autumn Flower*); Sp, 1977; (Olea); José Sacristán; *Variety* 4.10.78, p. 22

Home; USA, 1978; (Hammer); *Film Reader* no. 5 1982, p. 65

Home-Made Melodrama; GB, 1982; (Duckworth); Lyndey Stanley, Joy Chamberlain, Cass Bream; *MFB* 49, p. 87

homme à tout faire, L'; Can, 1980; (Lanctôt); Marcel Sabourin; *Variety* 2.4.80, p. 26

Hommes entre eux; Fr, 1976; (Terry); *La revue du cinéma* no. 353 1980, p. 98

Homo-Satisfactions; Fr, 1978; (Archenoul); *La revue du cinéma* no. 353 1980, p. 98

Homosexual Desire in Minnesota; USA, 1982 S8; (Hubbard)

Homosexuals; GB, 1966; (Butler); *BNFC* Mar 1967

Homosexuals on the March; USA, 1970?; (Rocco); Siebenand, p. 58 (see also *Mondo Rocco*)

Homovies; Fr, 1977; (Beauvais)

Hot Line; USA, 1970; (Goetz); Lois Lane, Rita Joyce; *AFIC* F6, p. 492

Hot Potato (see *La Patata Bollente*)

House of Pain and Pleasure; USA, 1969; (Rotsler); Vincene Wallace; *AFIC* F6, p. 499

How to Be a Homosexual; USA; (Jacoby); *CinémAction* no. 15 1981, p. 163

How the Hell Are You?; USA, S8; (Soul)

Hunger, The; USA, 1983; (Scott); Catherine Deneuve, Susan Sarandon; *MFB* 50, p. 100

Hure und Hurensohn, Die (*Dirty Daughters*); Ger, 1982; (Beiersdorf); Lothar Lambert; *Variety* 24.3.82, p. 108

Hurrycan; Ger, 1979; (Kekes); Christa Brands, Birger Bustorff

I Am Curious Gay (*Happy Birthday, Davy*); USA; 1970; (Fontaine); Chuck Roy, Larry Neilson; *AFIC* F6, p. 452

I Am Furious; USA, 1969; (Patrick); Maynard; *AFIC* F6, p. 514

Il était une fois un homosexuel; Fr, 1979; (Terry); Philippe Veschi, Swen Goteberg; *Altro Cinema* no. 30-31 1981, p. 333

I Love His Legs; USA, 1974?; (Eastman/McNeil); Dennis Dike; *Hollywood Reporter* 27.3.75, p. 15

Images; USA, 1982 video; (Carrol?)

Immacolata and Concetta; It, 1980; (Piscicelli); Ida de Benedetto, Marcella Michelangeli; *Variety* 21.5.80, p. 20

In Black and White (see *Nuance*)

In Contextus; Fr, 1977 S8; (Marti); *CinémAction* no. 15 1981, p. 161

In Memoriam; GB, 1982 S8; (de Florence); Thomas Mutke

Inside Story: Coming Out; GB, 1981 mtv; (Barber); *BNFC* vol. 19 1981, p. 41

Interdits (see *Milan Bleu, La confesse, Scopitone*)

International House; USA, 1933; (Sutherland); Franklin Pangborn; Russo, pp. 40-41

Interview with Arlene Raven; USA? video; (Blumenthal/Bowen)

In the Glitter Palace; USA, 1977 mtv; (Butler); Barbara Hershey; *Hollywood Reporter* 25.2.77, p. 8

In the Pictures; USA? video; (Mallory-Jones)

Intrigues de Sylvia Couski, Les; Fr, 1973; (Arrietta); Marie-France; *Ecran* no. 36 1975, p. 76
I Want to Be a Woman (see *Cambio de Sexo*)
I Was/I Am; USA; (Hammer); Barbara Hammer; *Jump Cut* no. 24-25 1981, p. 27
Ixé; Fr, 1980; (Soukaz); Philippe Veschi; *La revue du cinéma* Nov 1982, p. 65

Jack and Jill; USA, 1982 video; (Pignot/Smith); Alred Pignot, Jane Smith
Jean-Marc Pouvreur; Belg, 1980 S8; (Wouters); *CinémAction* no. 15 1981, p. 160
Jenny; Austr, 1980; Jenny, Amanda
Je suis un homo comme ils aiment; Fr, 1977; (Archenoul); *La revue du cinéma* no. 353 1980, p. 98
Jeunes proies pour mauvais garcons; Fr, 1977; (Terry); *La revue du cinéma* no. 353 1980, p. 98
Jim and Vern; USA; (Sutton); *CinémAction* no. 15 1981, p. 163
jocondes, Les; Fr, 1982; (Pillaut); Diane Lahumiere, Marie Agnes Then; *Variety* 25.8.82, p. 15
Johan; Fr, 1976; (Vallois); Patrice Pascal, Christine Weill; *Variety* 21.7.76, p. 22
John Linquist, Photographer of the Dance; USA, 1981; (Brodsky/Treadway)
Johnny Eagle; USA, 198-video; (Baron Infinity Mind?)
Journal filmé; Fr, 197-S8; (Morder); *CinémAction* no. 15 1981, pp. 109 - 114
journee particuliere, Une; Can; (Scola)
Judy's Front Room; GB, 1982 S8; (Homophlix); Myra
Julieta (see *Las Lesbianas y la Caliente Nina Julieta*)
Justcoeur; Can, 1980; (Stephens); Corrine Lanselle; *GN* 248, p. 46

Karlekens Sprak 2 (*Language of Love 2*); Swed, 1983; (Wickman); Inge Hegeler; *MFB* 50, p. 100
Kat; USA, 1978; (Warrenbrand)
King, The; USA, 1968; (Bear); Lisa St. Shaw, King Drummond; *AFIC* F6, p. 576
Kiss, The; USA, 1970?; (Rocco); Siebenand, p. 58 (see also *Mondo Rocco*)
Kiyampu; Jap, 1971; (Okabé); *CinémAction* no. 15 1981, p. 163
Klappe; Ger, 1980 video; (Stamkoski)
Kunstlife; USA; (Jacoby); *CinémAction* no. 15 1981, p. 156
Kustom Kar Kommando; USA, 1965; (Anger); *BNFC* Mar 1972

Labra; It, 1978 S8; (FFAG); *CinémAction* no. 15 1981, p. 163
Labyrinth; Ger/It, 1959; (Thiele); Nicole Badal; *MFB* 27, p. 24
Lambda Man; USA, 1980 S8; (Tartaglia); *CinémAction* no. 15 1981, p. 163
Laokoon und Sohn (*Laokoon and Sons*); Ger; (Ottinger); *GN* 191, p. v
Larking; (Segatto); *Body Politic* no. 64 1980, p. 37
Last Metro, The (see *La dernier métro*)
Late Show (see *Nachtvorstellungen*)
Laura; USA, 1944; (Preminger); Clifton Webb; *MFB* 11, p. 129
Laura, les ombres de l'étè (*Laura*); Fr, 1979; (Hamilton); Maud Adams, Dawn Dunlap; *MFB* 49, p. 87
Lavender Troubadour; USA, 1976 video; (Portland Video Access Project)
Lawless; USA; (Tartaglia); *CinémAction* no. 15 1981, pp. 154-155
Lebisia; USA, 1979; (van Syoc)
Legend of Valentino: A Romantic Fiction, The; USA, 1975 mtv; (Shavelson); Franco Nero; *Hollywood Reporter* 28.8.75, p. 6
Leonardo da Jason; USA, 1969; (Rocco); Siebenand, p. 58
Lesbianas y la Caliente Nina Julieta, Las (*Julieta*); Sp, 1982; (Bagram); Andrea Albani, Jorge Batalla; *Cineinforme* no. 108, p. 26
Lesbian Conference '73; USA, 1973 video; (Vulva Video)
Lesbian Mothers; USA, 197-video; (Amazon Media Project)
Lesbians; GB, 1966 mtv; (Phillips); *BNFC* Mar 1967

Lesbians; USA, 1975 video; (Portland NOW)
Lesbians Against the Right; Can, 1981 video
Lesbo; It, 1970; (Mulargia); Steven Ted, Carla Romanelli; *Intermezzo* no. 7-8 30.4.70,
    p. 10
Let Me Die a Woman; USA, 1978; Leo Wollman, Leslie; *MFB* 49, p. 230
Let There Be Boys (*Lonely Hunted, Free Soul, Tools of the Trade, Worlds Apart, Sun-
    day Sundae* as compilation film); USA, 1967; (Pierce); Ron Dilly, Pat Rocco; *AFIC*
    F6, p. 608
Lettre d'amour en somalie; Fr, 1982; (Mitterand)
Lianna; USA, 1983; (Sayles); Linda Griffiths, Jane Halleren; *Variety* 26.1.83, p. 14
Liebe wie andere auch, Eine (*A Love Like Any Other*); Ger, 1982; (Ripkens/Stempel);
    Stuart Wolfe, Klaus Adler
Lieve Jongens (*Dear Boys*); Neths, 1980; (Lussanet); Hugo Metsers, Hans Dagelet; *MFB*
    49, p. 64
Lift Off; USA, 198-video; (Graber/Smith)
Light from the Second Story Window; USA, 1973; (Allen); David Allen, Ray Todd; *Va-
    riety* 5.9.73, p. 6
Like Mack; USA, 1968; (Rocco); Siebenand, p. 58
Limitless Place, A (see *El Lugar sin Limites*)
Line of Apogee; USA, 1964-67; (Williams); *AFIC* F6 p. 615
Linsay Kemp; Belg, 1979 S8; (Wouters); *CinémAction* no. 15 1981, p. 160
Little Brother; GB, 1982 S8; (Carter)
Lives 1,2,3,4; USA, 197-video; (Orvino/Spencer)
Liv og Død (*Life and Death*); Nor, 1980; (Vennerød/Wam); Aundum Meling, Bjorn
    Skagestadt; *GN* 211, p. v
Loads; USA, 1980; (McDowell); *MFB* 49, p. 53
Looking for Mr. Goodbar; USA, 1977; (Brooks); Tom Berenger; *MFB* 45, p. 49
Lonely Hunted (see *Let There Be Boys*)
Long Good Friday, The; GB, 1979; (MacKenzie); Paul Freeman; *MFB* 48, p. 51
Lord Is My Shepherd - and He Knows I'm Gay, The; GB, 1973 mtv; (Deakin); Alan
    Whicker; *BNFC* vol. 16 1978, p. 41
Loss of Innocence (*The Greengage Summer*); GB, 1961; (Gilbert); Danielle Darrieux,
    Claude Nollier; *MFB* 28, p. 60
Lost Love: Another Senseless Tragedy; USA, 1981; (Zheutlin)
Love Is Blue; USA, 1968; (Rocco); Siebenand, pp. 16, 57
Love Like Any Other, A (see *Eine Liebe wie andere auch*)
Love Thing; USA?; (Mannetta); Joaquin La Habana
Louise Nevelson Takes a Bath; USA, 1983 video; (Walters)
Luckiest Guy in Town; USA, 1969? (Rocco); Siebenand, p. 58
Lueurs; Can, 1982 S8; (Gamache)
Lugar sin Limites, El (*A Limitless Place*); Mex, 1978; (Ripstein); Lucha Villa, Roberto
    Cobo; *Variety* 4.10.78, p. 22
Luna India; Fr, 1976 S8; (Hernandez); *CinémAction* no. 15 1981, p. 160
Luna Tune; USA, 1977; (Clement); *CinémAction no. 15 1981, p. 163*
Lunch; USA, 1974; (McDowell); Velvet Busch, Mark Ellinger
Lust in the Afternoon; USA, 1970; (DeSimone); Siebenand, p. 108
Lysistrata; USA, 1968; (Matt); *AFIC* F6, p. 652

Madame X; Ger, 1977; (Ottinger); Tabea Blumenschein, Roswitha Jantz; *Time Out* no.
    456 12-18.1.79, pp. 35,37
Madam of Many Faces; USA, 198-video; (Davis)
Madonna and Child; GB, 1980; (Davies); Terry O'Sullivan, Sheila Raynor; *MFB* 48, p.
    210
Magic in the Raw; USA, 1969; (Rocco); Siebenand, p. 58
Maidens; Austr, 1979; (Thornley); Jeni Thornley; *FilmNews* (Austr) vol. 8 no. 9 1978,
    p. 16

maison qui empêche de voir la ville, La; Can, 1974; (Audy); *Copie Zero* no. 11 1981, pp. 24-25

Making Love; USA, 1982; (Hiller); Michael Ontkean, Harry Hamlin; *MFB* 49. p. 88

Male Groupie; USA: (DeSimone); Siebenand, p. 93

Males hard corps; Fr, 1977; (Terry); Jean Estienne, Michel Werner; *Ecran* no. 62 1977, p. 67

Male Techniques; USA, 1970; *AFIC* F6, p. 671

Malizia erotica (And Give Us Our Daily Sex); It/Sp?, 1980; (Larraz); Laura Gemser, Barbara Rey; *MFB* 47, p. 5

Man and Man; USA, 1970; *AFIC* F6, p. 672

Manderley; Sp, 1980; (Garay); José Ocaña, Enrique Rada; *GN* 211, p. v

Man Called Autumn Flower, A (see *Un Hombre Llamado Flor de Otoño*)

Man - Eight Girls, A; USA, 1968; Andrea Castelmagne, Robin Burnee; *AFIC* F6, p. 674

Manic, a Love Story; USA, 1981 S8; (Hadden)

marche gay, Le (Washington Gay Pride March); Fr, 1980 S8?; (Soukaz)

March On!; USA, 1979 S8; (Hubbard)

March on Washington; USA, 1979 video; (Fury/Reeter/ Rivchin)

Mare Nostrum; USA, 1926; (Ingram); Madame Pasquerette, Alice Terry; *GN* 196, p. 26

Marianne and Moya; USA, 1977; (Mersky)

Mario Banana; USA, 1964; (Warhol); Mario Montez

Mars au matin; Can, 1982 S8; (Jacob)

Martin (The Executioner); Nor, 1980; (Risan); Unnl Evjan; *GN* 211, p. v

Mason's Life; USA, 1979; (Lowy); *CinémAction* no. 15 1981, p. 163

Mass; USA, 1980 video; (Riddler); Catherine Feleppa, Karin Koebergen

Matter of Life, A; USA, 1969; (Rocco); Siebenand, p. 58

Mattutino; It, 1975 S8; (Amidiei); *CinémAction* no. 15 1981, p. 163

maudits, Les (The Damned); Fr, 1947; (Clément); Michel Auclair; *MFB* 16, p. 193/Russo, p. 249

Max-Out: USA, 1970; (Kaylor); Mel Rivers, Joe Rizzo; *AFIC* F6, p. 696

Maynila, Sa Mga Kuko Ng Liwang (Manila, in the Claws of Darkness); Phil, 1975; (Brocka); Rafael Roco Jnr., Jojo Abella; *MFB* 48, p. 117

Me and My Brother; USA, 1965?; (Frank); Julius Orlovsky, Allen Ginsberg; *AFIC* F6, p. 696

Meanwhile, Back in the City...; GB, 1983 S8; (Bell)

Meat Market Arrest; USA, 1970?; (Rocco); Siebenand, p. 58 (see also *Mondo Rocco*)

Meet the Sex; USA, 1969; *AFIC* F6, p. 698

menage moderne du Madame Butterfly, La; Fr, 1925-35; *Body Politic* no. 90 1983, p. 30

Menses; USA, 1974; (Hammer); *Film Reader* no. 5 1982, p. 61

Merry Christmas, Mr. Lawrence; GB, 1982; (Oshima); David Bowie, Ryuichi Sakamoto, Johnny Okura; *MFB* 50, p. 121

Me Show, The; USA, 1983 video; (Canaly); Noel Day, Gina Roman, Peter Stack

Michael, a Gay Son; Can, 1981; (Glawson); *Body Politic* Feb 1981

Mid-Boy; USA, 1969; (Rocco); Siebenand, p. 58

Midnight Man, The; USA, 1974; (Kibbee/Lancaster); Susan Clark, Catherine Bach; *MFB* 42, p. 12

Milan Bleu (see *Interdits*)

Mimi la Douce; USA, 1968; *AFIC* F6, p. 706

Miskhak Makhbuim (Hide and Seek); Is, 1980; (Wolman); Dorn Tavori, Musbach Elchalawani; *Variety* 25.6.80, p. 21

Miss 'Ogynie et les hommes-fleurs; Belg, 1973; (Pavel); Martine Kelly; *Variety* 8.5.74, p. 37

Modesty Blaise; GB, 1966; (Losey); Dirk Bogarde; *MFB* 33, p. 89

Moments; Fr/Is, 1979; (Bat-Adam); Michel Bat-Adam, Brigitte Cabillon

Monday Morning Pronouns; USA, 1979 S8; (Dickoff)

Mondo Rocco (Homosexuals on the March, Meat Market Arrest, Groovy Guy 1969, Screen

Test, The Kiss, A Night at Joani's as compilation film); USA, 1970; (Rocco); *AFIC* F6, p. 722
Mondo Trasho; USA, 1969; (Waters); Divine, Mary Vivian Pearce; *Variety* 11.2.70, p. 16
Moon Goddess; USA, 1976; (Hammer); Barbara Hammer, Gloria Churchman; *Film Reader* no. 5 1982, p. 62
Morris Loves Jack; Austr, 1979; (Hofmann); John Hargreaves, Bill Hunter; *Cinema Papers* no. 24 Dec 1979-Jan 1980, pp. 662-663
Muchachas de Uniforme; Mex, 1950; (Crevenna); *Altro Cinema* no. 30-31 1981, p. 13
Multiple Maniacs; USA, 1970; (Waters); Divine, Mink Stole; *GN* 238, p. 23
Multiple Orgasm; USA; (Hammer)
Murder; GB, 1930; (Hitchcock); Esme Perry; *MFB* 42, p. 165
Musclebound; USA, 197-; (Brown); *GN* 175
Muscle Lens; GB, 1983 S8; (Farrer)
musée, Le; Fr, 1976; (Deveau); *CinémAction* no. 15 1981, p. 162
Music from the Heart; USA, 1976; (Karp/Nixon/Whitaker)

Nachtvorstellungen (Late Show); Ger, 1978; (Lambert); Dagmar Beiersdorf, Cihan Anasai; *Variety* 28.6.78
Naked Civil Servant, The; GB, 1975 mtv; (Gold); John Hurt; *GN* 86, p. 19
Naked Summer; USA, 1969; (Rocco); Siebenand, p. 58
Nanami: Inferno of First Love (see *Hatsukoi jigokuhen*)
Navy Blue; USA, 197-; (Ellie); George Payne, Jack Wrangler; *GN* 175
Nea; Fr/Ger, 1976; (Kaplan); Samy Frey, Ann Zacharias; *MFB* 44, p. 263
New Anti-Life Force, The; Ger, 1980 S8; (Funke/ Leopold)
New Barbarians, The (see *I nuovi barbari*)
New York after Midnight; USA, 1980; (Scandalari); Russo, p. 238
New York Experience (see *Now or Never*)
Next Stop, Greenwich Village; USA, 1975; (Mazursky); Antonio Fargas; *MFB* 44, p. 27
Nick and John; USA; (Dundas); *CinémAction* no. 15 1981, p. 164
Night at Joani's, A; USA, 1970?; (Rocco); Siebenand, p. 58 (see also *Mondo Rocco*)
Night Moves; NZ, 1979; (Turner); Robert Shannon, Paul Eady; *New Zealand Film* no. 4 1979, p. 2
Night Shift; USA; (Hallis); *CinémAction* no. 15 1981, p. 164
Nijinsky; USA, 1980; (Ross); Alan Bates, George de la Peña; *MFB* 47, p. 114
Nikutai no gakko (School of Love); Jap, 1965; (Kinoshita); Tsutomu Yamazaki; *AFIC* F6, p. 944
No Exit; USA/Arg, 1962; (Danielewski); Viveca Lindfors; *AFIC* F6, p. 775
Nothing Personal; GB, 1980; (Moule/Morris)
Novia ensangrentada, La (The Blood-Spattered Bride); Sp, 1972; (Aranda); Maribel Martin, Alexandra Bastardo; *MFB* 47, p. 138
Now or Never (New York Experience); Ger, 1979; (Lambert); Sylvia Heidermann, Tally Brown; *Variety* 15.8.79, p. 25
Nuance (In Black and White); Can, 1979; (McGarry)
Nudes, a Sketchbook; USA, 1974; (McDowell); Hugo, Mark; *MFB* 49, p. 53
nuovi barbari, I (The New Barbarians); It, 1983; (Castellari); Luigi Montefiori; *MFB* 50, p. 219

Oblivion; USA, 1969; (Chomont); *Millennium Film Journal* no. 3, pp. 122-125
Ocaño, retrat intermitent (Ocaño, a Gay Portrait); Sp, 1978; (Pons); José Perez Ocaño; *Variety* 24.5.78, p. 40
Off/On Wall; Ger, 1977 video; (Speck)
oiseaux de nuit, Les; Fr, 1977; (Barnier/Lasfragues); *Ecran* no. 66 1978, pp. 56-57
Ommossessualita: Ovvero Diversi in Periferia; It, 1978; (Rapetti)
On a Cold Afternoon; USA; (Jabaily); *CinémAction* no. 15 1981, p. 164
One Touching One; USA, 1970; (Eden); *AFIC* F6, p. 803

Onion Field, The; USA, 1979; (Becker); James Woods; *MFB* 47, p. 51
Only a Test; USA, 1983, video; (Wilson/Simons)
Only When I Laugh; USA, 1981; (Jordan); James Coco; *MFB* 49, p. 7
Only Yesterday; USA, 1933; (Stahl); Franklin Pangborn, Barry Norton; Russo, pp. 41-42
Onna onna onna monogatari (Women...Oh, Women!); Jap, 1963; (Takechi); *AFIC* F6, p. 1241
On the Beach; USA, 1978; (Mitera)
Order, The; USA, 198-video; (Manfredini); Joy Lieberman, Susan Regeski
Other Woman, The; USA, 1982 video; (McMurphy/Dorr); Strawn Bovee, Jamielle Stanley
Our Trip; USA; (Hammer)

Paradis perdu; Fr, 1978; (Prenant); *CinémAction* no. 15 1981, p. 162
Paradox of the Mermaids (see *Unding Undine*)
Parasite Murders, The (see *Shivers*)
Parents of Gays; Austr, 198-video
Partners; USA, 1982; (Burrows); John Hurt; *MFB* 49, p. 135
Passage; USA, 1981 S8; (Picard)
Passing Strangers; USA, 1974; (Bressan)
Patata Bollente, La (Hot Potato); It, 1979; (Vanzina); Renato Pozetto, Edwige Fenech; *Variety* 20.2.80, p. 26
Paulines Geburtstag oder Die Bestie von Notre Dame; Ger, 1979; (Mattheis); Harry Pauly, Jochen Pehrs; *Filmecho/Filmwoche* no. 59-60 26.10.79, p. 12
Peepshow; Ger, 1980; (Stamkoski)
Perfect Couple, A; USA, 1979; (Altman); Meredith McRae, Tomi-Lee Bradley; *MFB* 46, p. 231
Performance; USA, 1969; (Rocco); Siebenand, p. 58
Personal Best; USA, 1982; (Towne); Mariel Hemingway, Patrice Donnelly; *MFB* 50, p. 193
Peter the Peeker; USA, 1970; (DeSimone); Siebenand, p. 108
P4W: Prison for Women; Can, 1981; (Dale/Cole); *Variety* 9.9.81, p. 22
phallophiles, Les; Fr, 1979; (Terry); *La revue du cinéma* no. 353 1980, p. 98
Pick-Up Girls (see *La chica de las bragas transparentes*)
Picnic in the Park; USA, 1969?; (Rocco); Siebenand, p. 58
Pier Groups; USA, 197-; (Brown); Keith Anthoni, Johnny Kovaks; *GN* 175
Pink Triangle; USA, 1982; (Pink Triangles Collective)
Pink Triangles Rising; USA, 1982 video; (Dinello/Corboy)
Pixote a lei do mais fraco (Pixote); Braz, 1981; (Babenco); Jorge Juliao, Gilberto Moura; *MFB* 50, p. 19
Place Between Our Bodies, The; USA?, 1975; (Wallin)
plouffe, Les; Can, 1981; (Carle); Gabriel Arcand; *Variety* 29.4.81, p. 19
Plusieurs tombent en amour (Some Even Fall in Love); Can, 1979; (Simoneau); *Copie Zero* no. 7 1979, pp. 27-28
polygame, Le; Fr, 1971; (Terry); *Film Francais* 24.8.73, p. 10
Pornographie chez Madame Saint-Claude; Fr, 1975; (Terry); Erika Cool, Liane Lautrec; *Ecran* no. 42 1975, p. 71
Posing; GB, 1979; (collective)
Possession du condamne; (Lheureux); Belg, 1967; Luc Alexandre, Gilles Brenta
Prisms; USA; (Seligman); *CinémAction* no. 15 1981, p. 164
Prisoner, The; USA, 1970?; (Rocco); Siebenand, p. 58
Private Benjamin; USA, 1980; (Zieff); Eileen Brennan; *MFB* 48, p. 32
Privates on Parade; GB, 1982; (Blakemore); Denis Quilley; *MFB* 50, p. 47
Propaganda; Neths; (Dhondt); *CinémAction* no. 15 1981, p. 162
Psyche; USA, 1948; (Markopoulos)
Psychosynthesis; USA, 1975; (Hammer); Barbara Hammer; *Film Reader* no. 5 1982, pp. 61-62
Public; USA, 1981 S8; (Dong)

Pull My Daisy; USA, 1959; (Frank/Lesley); Allen Ginsberg, Mooney Peebles; *MFB* 41, p. 17

Puzzle of a Downfall Child; USA, 1970; (Schatzberg); Viveca Lindfors; *MFB* 10, p. 211

Quartetto Basileus, Il (The Basel Quartet); It, 1982; (Carpi); Michel Vitold; *Variety* 25.8.82, p. 15

Querelle; Ger, 1982; (Fassbinder); Franco Nero, Brad Davis; *MFB* 50, p.

Question of Love; USA, 1978 mtv; (Thorpe); Gena Rowlands, Jane Alexander; *Hollywood Reporter* 27.11.78, p. 4

Rapunzel Let Your Hair Down; GB, 1978; (Shapiro/ Ronay/Winham); *MFB* 45, p. 245

Reclining Cowboy; USA, 1969?; (Rocco); Siebenand, p. 58

Reflections in a Muddy Pool; USA, 1969; (Rocco); Siebenand, p. 58

Reflexive Francis Film; USA, 1976; (Rappaport); Francis Moyer, Mark Gurvitz; *BNFC* 1982, p. 131

rendez-vous d'Anna, Les; Fr/Belg/Ger, 1978; (Akerman); Aurore Clément, Helmut Griem; *MFB* 47, p. 139

Rennie; USA; (Norman); *CinémAction* no. 15 1981, p. 164

Richard's Things; GB, 1980; (Harvey); Liv Ullman, Amanda Redman; *Variety* 10.9.80, p. 36

Rivales; Ger, 1979 S8; (Bockmayer); *CinémAction* no. 15 1981, p. 160

Robin Crusoe; USA, 1968; *AFIC* F6, p. 914

Roman Tidbits (see *Tales for Males*)

Ronnie; USA, 1973; (McDowell); *MFB* 49, p. 53

Room, The; USA, 1970?; (Rocco); Siebenand, p. 58

Rosa Winkel? Das ist doch schon lange vorbei; Ger, 1976; (Stoffel)

Rote Liebe; Ger, 1982; (Praunheim); Sasha Hammer, Eddie Constantine; *Variety* 17.3.82, p. 166

Rudd Family Goes to Town, The (see *Dad and Dave Come to Town*)

Runnin' After Love; Braz, 1980; (Christensen); Wagner Montes; *Mandate* vol. 6 no. 63 1980, pp. 26-27

Sabre Dance (see *Tales for Males*)

Sailor and the Leather Stud; USA, 1969; (Rocco); Siebenand, p. 58

Sailor at Large; USA, 1968; (Rocco); Siebenand, p. 58

St. Genet martyr et poete; Fr, 1976; (Gilles); *CinémAction* no. 15 1981, p. 162

Salamandre, Le; It, 1969; (Cavallone); Erna Schurer, Beryl Cunningham; *Cinema d'Oggi* 10.3.69, p. 3

Salome; Fr, 1975 S8; (Hernandez); *CinémAction* no. 15 1981, p. 162

Salome; Gr; (Mouratidis); *CinémAction* no. 15 1981, p. 162

Salut, a mardi; Fr, 1980 S8; (Moizeau); *CinémAction* no. 15 1981, p. 162

San Francisco Gay Freedom Gay; USA, 1980 video; (Esteeves)

Sappho; USA, 1978; (Hammer)

Satan bouche un coin; Belg, 1977; (Bouyxou); *CinémAction* no. 15 1981, p. 160

School of Love (see *Nikutai no gakko*)

Scopitone (see *Interdits*)

Screen Test; USA, 1970?; (Rocco); Jim Cassidy, Brian Reynolds; Siebenand, pp. 58, 79 (see also *Mondo Rocco*)

Scrubbers; GB, 1982; (Zetterling); Amanda York, Kate Ingram; *MFB* 49, p. 272

Secret Policeman's Other Ball, The; GB, 1982; (Temple); Alan Bennett, John Fortune; *MFB* 49, p. 69

Separate Piece, A; USA, 1972; (Peerce); Parker Stevenson, John Heyl; *Variety* 13.9.72, p. 20

Sergeant Matlovitch vs. the US Air Force; USA, 1978 mtv; (Leaf); Brad Dourif; *Hollywood Reporter* 21.7.77, p. 13

7 images impossible; Belg, 1979 S8; (Maglengreau); *CinémAction* no. 15 1981, p. 160

Sextool; USA, 1975; (Halsted); Charmaine Lee Anderson, Divine; Siebenand, pp. 194-199, 315-320/ *Variety* 12.3.75, p. 20
Sexual I.D.; USA, 198-video; (Maurier?)
Sexual Fantasy Conference; USA, 1973 video; (Ripp)
Sfratto Nelo Spazia; It, 1980; (Melano); *CinémAction* no. 15 1981, pp. 137-140
Shadow Box, The; USA, 1980 mtv; (Newman); Christopher Plummer, Ben Masters
Shame, Shame, Everybody Knows Her Name; USA, 1969; (Jacoby); Getti Miller; *AFIC* F6, p. 975
Sharing the Secret; Can, 1981 mtv; (Kastner)
She Mob; USA, 1968; Marni Castle; *AFIC* F6, p. 978
Shivers (The Parasite Murders); USA, 1974; (Cronenberg); Barbara Steele, Susan Petrie; *MFB* 43, p. 62
Shonen shiko; Jap, 1973; (Okabé); *CinémAction* no. 15 1981, p. 163
Sidney Shorr: A Girl's Best Friend ; USA, 1981 mtv; (Mayberry); Tony Randall; *Variety* 14.10.81, p. 318
Sign, The; USA, 1980; (Carr/Bartoni/Whitaker)
Sign of Fire (see *Feuerzeichen*)
Silencis (Silence); Sp, 1982; (Xavier)
Silverpoint; USA, 1974; (Linkevitch)
Showtime; Austr, 1978; (Chapman); Lorna Lesley, Jude Kuring; *FilmNews* (Austr) June 1978, p. 11
Simone Barbès ou la vertu (Simone Barbès, or Virtue); Fr, 1979; (Treilhou); Ingrid Bourgoin, Martine Simonet; *Variety* 7.5.80, p. 576
Sister Ray; Ger, 1980 S8; (Schier/Bässmann/Vivian)
Sisters in Leather; USA, 1969; (Crilly aka Spencer); Pat Barrington; *AFIC* F6, p. 994
Sisters Snow; Sp, 1979 S8; (5 QK collective); *CinémAction* no. 15 1981, p. 161
16-21-32; GB, 1983 S8; (Bell)
Skins; GB, 1982 2 x S8; (de Florence); Thomas Mutke, Bruno de Florence
Soilers, The; USA, 1923; (Roach); Stan Laurel, Oliver Hardy; Russo, pp. 25-26
So Many Men, So Little Time; USA, 197-; (Brown); Justin Thyme, Ed Stiffler; *GN* 175
Some American Feminists; Can, 1977; (Guilbeault/ Brossard/Wescott); Rita Mae Brown; *MFB* 48, p. 161
Some Even Fall in Love (see *Plusieurs tombent en amour*)
Some of these Stories are True; USA, 1981 video; (Adair)
Song of the Godbody; USA, 1977; (Broughton); *CinémAction* no. 15 1981, p. 156
Son of the Family; USA; (Selway); *CinémAction* no. 15 1981, p. 165
Sons of Satan; USA, 1973; (DeSimone); Siebenand, p. 109
Sound of Fast Relief, The (see *Das Gerausch rasche Erlösung*)
Specialists, The; 1968; (Moser); Ina Albrect, Sylvia Koerner; *AFIC* F6, p. 1017
Spetters; Neths, 1980; (Verhoeven); Toon Agterberg, Martin Spanjer; *Variety* 2.4.80, p. 22
Spirit of Greenham; GB, 1983 S8; (Carter)
Squeeze; NZ, 1980; (Turner); Paul Eady, Robert Shannon; *Variety* 3.12.80, p. 22
Stadt der verlorenen Seelen (City of Lost Souls/Berlin Blues); Ger, 1983; (Praunheim); Angie Stardust, Tron van Bergdorfe; *Variety* 16.3.83, p. 23
STA Men; USA; (Benson); *CinémAction* no. 15 1981, p. 165
Station to Station; USA, 1974; (DeSimone); Siebenand, pp. 88-89
Stop the Movie Cruising!; USA, 1979 S8; (Hubbard)
Story of No Importance; Fr, 1980; (Duron)
Strange One, The (see *End as a Man*)
Strawberry Blonde (see *Bionda Fragola*)
Strega; USA, 1981 S8; (Picard)
Strip-Strip; USA, 1968; (Rocco); Siebenand, p. 58
Strip-Tease/Vermine; Can, 1980 video; (Paradis); *CinémAction* no. 15 1981, p. 160
Stud Farm, The; USA, 1969; (Zacha); Gary Yuma, Wayne Douglas; *AFIC* F6, p. 1040
Subway Riders; USA, 1981; (Poe); Cookie Mueller; *MFB* 50, p. 195

Summer Lovers; USA, 1982; (Kleiser); Daryl Hannah, Valerie Quennessen; *MFB* 49, p. 294

Sunday Sundae (see *Let There Be Boys*)

Sunny Boys; USA, 1968; (Rocco); Siebenand, p. 58

Superdyke; USA; (Hammer)

Superdyke Meets Madame X; USA; (Hammer/Almy)

Surprise Lover; USA, 1969; (Rocco); Siebenand, p. 58

Surprise of a Knight; USA, 192-; (Wild); *Body Politic* no. 90 1983, p. 30

Susana; USA, 1979; (Blaustein); *Jump Cut* no. 28, pp. 43-44

Sweet Body of Bianca; Gr?, 1982; (Milonako); Marina Frajese, Sabrina Mastrolorenzi; *MFB* 50, p. 167

Sweet Dreams; USA, 1969; (Avildsen); *American Cinematographer* Aug 1970, p. 762

Sweet Taste of Youth, A; USA, 1972; (Knight); Siebenand, p. 124

aboo (the Single and the LP); USA, 1980; (McDowell); George Kuchar, Marion Eaton; *MFB* 49, p. 49

Take, Retake; GB, 1983 S8; (Lindy)

Tales for Males (Roman Tidbits, Always on Sundays, Discobolos, Sabre Dance as compilation film); USA, 1970; *AFIC* F6, p. 1063

Talk Naughty To Me; USA, 1980; (Warfield); John Leslie, Leslie Bovee; *MFB* 49, p. 92

Tarzan the Fearless; USA, 1970; (DeSimone); Siebenand, p. 108

tasse, La; Fr, 1975 S8; (Nedjar); *CinémAction* no. 15 1981, p. 162

Taxi zum Klo (Taxi to the Loo); Ger, 1980; (Ripploh); Frank Ripploh, Bernd Broaderup; *MFB* 49, p. 11

télégraphiste, Le; Fr, 1921-26; *Body Politic* no. 90 1983, p. 30

Tendre et voyou; Fr, 1978; (Archenoul); *La revue du cinéma* no. 353 1980, p. 98

Tendre et voyou; Fr, 1979; (Barsakoff); Alain Vallès, Omar Habib; *Altro Cinema* no. 30-31 1981, p. 34

tête de Normande St-Onge, La; Can, 1975; (Carle); Carol Laure; *Variety* 19.5.76, p. 23

Thank You, Masked Man; USA, 1967; (Bruce?); Lenny Bruce; Russo, p. 258

That's About the Size of It; USA, 1968; (Rocco); Siebenand, p. 58

That's the Story of My Life; Neths; (de Vries); *CinémAction* no. 15 1981, p. 162

That Tender Touch; USA, 1969; (Vincent); Sue Bernard, Bee Tompkins; *AFIC* F6, p. 1084

There is More to Howard than Meets the Eye; GB, 1982 S8; (de Florence)

Three Comrades; USA, 192-; *Body Politic* no. 90 1983, p. 30

Three on a Spree; USA, 1969; (Rocco); Siebenand, p. 58

3 People/New York/1974; USA, 1974?; (Rapaport); *CinémAction* no. 15 1981, p. 165

Three's a Crowd; USA, 1969; (Rocco); Siebenand, p. 58

Three Short Episodes; GB, 1980; (Finkelstein)

Three Women; USA, 1975 video; (Korsts)

Thrilling; GB, 1983 S8; (Bennett)

Tiergarten; Ger, 1980; (Lambert); Steven Adamczewski, Dagmar Beiersdorf; *Variety* 5.3.80, p. 28

Together; USA, 1975; (Broughton/Singer)

Toni, Randi and Marie; Can, 1974; (Hallis); Toni, Randi; *Cinema Canada* no. 27 1976, p. 55

Too Good to Be True?; GB, 1979; (Gold); Tom Robinson; *BNFC* vol. 18 1980, p. 127

Tools of the Trade (see *Let There Be Boys*)

Tortures That Laugh; GB, 1981 S8; (Maybury)

Tous les garcons; Can, 1981 S8; (Laberge)

Track Two; Can, 1981; (Sutherland/Lemmon/Keith); *Variety* 23.3.83, p. 22

Traviata, La; Ger, 1978 S8; (Bockmayer); *CinémAction* no. 15 1981, p. 160

Tread Softly; Austr, 1980; (Drew); Robyn Nevin, Natalie Bate; *GN* 211, p. v

Trick and the Trade; USA, 1970; *AFIC* F6, p. 1134

Trouble-fête; Can, 1965; (Patry); Lucien Hamilton; *Variety* 20.5.64, p. 6

Truck It; USA, 1973; (Halsted); Jim Frost; *Variety* 21.2.73, p. 24
True Romance etc.; GB, 1982; (Newsreel Collective); Isiaka Amodu; *MFB* 49, p. 98
truite, La (The Trout); Fr, 1982; (Losey); Jean-Pierre Cassel, Jacques Spiesser; *Variety* 15.9.82, p. 13
Two Lions in the Sun (see *Deux lions au soleil*)
T-WO-MEN; Fr, 1972; (Neke); *Time Out* no. 489 31.8-6.9.79, p. 51

Ultravixens (see *Beneath the Valley of the Ultravixens*)
Undressed for the Occasion; USA, 1969?; (Rocco); Siebenand, p. 58
Underground USA; USA, 1980; (Mitchell); Eric Mitchell; *MFB* 48, p. 120
Unding Undine (Paradox of the Mermaids); Ger, 1980; (Funke-Stern/Leopold)
Une, deux, trois; Can, 1978 S8; (Anderson)
Unity; USA, 1978; (Huestis); *CinémAction* no. 15 1981, p. 165
Untitled; USA; (Heller); *CinémAction* no. 15 1981, p. 165
Up; USA, 1976; (Meyer); Janet Wood, Robert McLane; *MFB* 48, p. 98
Upstairs Room, The; USA, 1970; (DeSimone); Scot Arden, Joey Latti; *AFIC* F6, p. 1164
Up, Up and Now; USA, 1969; (Rocco); Siebenand, p. 58

vent souffle ou il veut, Le; Fr, 1973; (Danel); *CinémAction* no. 15 1981, p. 162
Verdammte Stadt (Fucking City); Ger, 1982; (Lambert); Lothar Lambert; *Variety* 30.12.81, p. 18
Veronica 4 Rose; GB, 1982 mtv; (Chait)
Very Special Friend, A; USA, 1969; (Rocco); Siebenand, p. 58
Victor/Victoria; GB, 1982; (Edwards); Robert Preston, Malcolm Jamieson; *MFB* 49, p. 71
Vierde Man, De (The Fourth Man); Neths, 1983; (Verhoeven); Jeroen Krabbé; *Variety* 27.4.83, p. 36
vie rêvée, La (Dream Life); Can, 1972; (Dansereau); Liliane Lemaître-Auger, Véronique le Flaguais; *MFB* 45, p. 208
Vingarne (The Wings); Swed, 1916; (Stiller); Egil Eide, Lars Hanson; Werner, pp. 312-324
Voices; USA, 1953; (Smitz); Siebenand, p. 14
voyage de l'ogre, Le; Can, 1981 video; (Paradis)
Vrouw als Eva, Een (A Woman Like Eve) Neths, 1979; Monique Van de Ven, Maria Schneider; *Variety* 26.3.80, p. 21

Walk a Crooked Path; GB, 1969; (Brason); Faith Brook, Tenniel Evans; *MFB* 37, p. 170
Walt Whitman; USA 1976 mtv
Wanted; USA, 1969; (Rocco); Siebenand, p. 58
Warrior's Husband, The; USA, 1933; (Lang); Ernest Truex; Russo, p. 39
War Widow, The; USA, 1976 mtv; (Bogart); Pamela Bellwood, Frances Lee McCain; *Hollywood Reporter* 28.10.76, p. 8
Watch Out, There's a Queer About; GB, 1981 video; (Lipman); Gordon McDonald; *BNFC* vol. 21 no. 1 1983, p. 11
We Are Ourselves; USA; (Hersey); *CinémAction* no. 15 1981, p. 165
Weisse Reise (White Journey); Fr/Switz, 1978-80; (Schroeter); Maria Schneider, Margareth Clementi; *Gn* 211, p. v
We're Alive; USA, 1974; (UCLA Women's Film Workshop/Video Workshop of California); *MFB* 49, p. 176
We Three; USA, 1969?; (Rocco); Siebenand, p. 58
Whatever Happened to Susan Jane?; USA, 1981; (Huestis); Ann Block, Francesca Rosa
Whatever Momma Wants; USA, 1972; (Hall); Siebenand, p. 109
What Really Happened to Baby Jane?; USA; (Harrison); Siebenand, p. 77
What You Take for Granted; USA, 1983; (Citron); Donna Blue Lachman
Wheeee; USA, 1969; (Rocco); Siebenand, p. 58
Wheel Dream; USA; (Jabaily); *CinémAction* no. 15 1981, p. 165
When the Cat's Away; USA, 1969; (Rocco); Siebenand, p. 58

Where Do We Go Now? *(AIDS)*; GB, 1982 S8?; (Julien)
Who Are We?; USA, 1977 mtv; (Adair); *Jump Cut* no. 16 1977, pp. 16-17
Who Happen to Be Gay; USA, 1981; (Beldin/Krenzien); *BNFC* 1982, p. 48
Who Killed Teddy Bear?; USA, 1965; (Cates); Elaine Strich; *Variety* 6.10.65, p. 6
Winter Kept Us Warm; Can, 1965; (Secter); *Body Politic* May 1982
Witches Faggots Dykes and Poofters; Austr, 1980; (One in Seven Collective); *MFB* 48, p. 164
Wive's Tale, A (see *Une histoire des femmes*)
Woman Next Door, The (see *La femme d'à côté*)
Women I Love; USA, 197-; (Hammer); *Jump Cut* no. 24-25 1981, p. 30
Women in Chains; USA, 1973 mtv; Barbara Luna; *Hollywood Reporter* 28.1.72, p. 25
Wonderful World of Guys; USA, 197-; (Hall); *GN* 175
World in Action: Gay Pride; GB, 1979 video/mtv; (Blake/Blake); Tom Robinson, Michael Mason; *BNFC* vol. 18 1980, p. 41
World of Light: A Portrait of May Sarton; USA; (Simpson/Wheelock); *CinémAction* no. 15 1981, p. 165
Worlds Apart (see *Let There Be Boys*)
Worst Crime of All!, The; USA, 1966; (Lamb); Cathy Crowfoot; *AFIC* F6, p. 1243

X; USA; (Hammer); Barbara Hammer; *Jump Cut* no. 24-25 1981, p. 27
Xmas; USA, 1969; *AFIC* F6, p. 1247
X, Y and Zee (see *Zee and Co.*)

Yahoo; USA, 1968; (Rocco); Siebenand, p. 58
Yes, We Have Changed; USA, 1982; (Kimmelman); *BNFC* vol. 21 1983

Zee and Co. *(X, Y and Zee)*; GB, 1971; (Hutton); Elizabeth Taylor, Susannah York; *MFB* 39, p. 82
Zorro the Gay Blade; USA, 1981; (Medak); George Hamilton; *MFB* 49, p. 12

BIBLIOGRAPHY

Introduction

I have not attempted anything like a comprehensive up-date of this bibliography since the first (1977) edition. There has been a considerable growth in film criticism in the gay press, much of it of a high quality (e.g., Jack Babuscio, Lee Atwell, Tom Waugh, Robin Wood—I am not aware of any lesbian critics regularly in the gay press). To include every such example would extend this bibliography inordinately, and rather than make invidious judgements as to 'lasting merit', I have restricted entries to pieces dealing at some length with a general topic (including the work of particular directors, actors, etc.)—in other words, I have not included reviews of single films, however thoughtful or important.

R.D. 1980

The recent so-called spate of Hollywood films that foreground gay characters has also inspired much writing on the subject. For this reason, reviews of single films have now been included where they reflect more widely on the representation of gay people. Otherwise, the previous decision not to list individual film reviews has been upheld in the desire for conciseness.

M.F. 1983

Altro Cinema, Rome, no. 30-31 July-Oct 1980 (entire issue devoted to articles on gays and film).

Atwell, Lee 'Homosexual Themes in the Cinema', *Tangents*, 1 (6), Mar 1966, pp. 4-10; 1 (7) Apr 1966, pp. 4-9; 'Visconti', *Gay Sunshine* 29-30; 'The Films of Pasolini', *Gay Sunshine* 28; 'Interview: Filmmaker Arthur Bressan' *Fag Rag/Gay Sunshine* combined summer issue 1974.

Avicolli, T. 'Rosa von Praunheim: Controversial Filmmaker' *Gay Community News,* Boston, May 20 1978.

Babuscio, Jack: articles in *Gay News*—.73 (gay men and 'camp women'), 74 (John Schlesinger), 75 (images of masculinity), 76 (hardporn), 78 (censorship), 79 (James Dean), 80 (Parker Tyler), 81 (sexual colonialism in the British cinema), 83 (repression and role-playing), 85 (Marilyn Monroe), 86 (gays and the military in film), 87 (Andy Warhol), 88 (Paul Morrissey), 89 (Oscar Wilde on screen), 90 (gay stereotypes), 91 (defining camp), 92 ('sissies'), 93 ('tomboys'), 94 (the prison genre), 100 (gays as villains), 102 (Dirk Bogarde), 103 (lesbian vampires), 104 (Montgomery Clift), 110 (gays in horror films), 111 (Carmen Miranda), 117 ('buddy movies'), 124 (parents of gays in films), 129/130 (pornography), 146 (Eisenstein), 158 (gays and race in films), 175 (American hardcore porn), 181 (Hitchcock), 183 (schoolgirls), 184 (schoolboys).

Bachstein, Heimo 'Anders Als Die Anderen: Homosexualität im Film' *Retro*, Munich, no. 16 July-Aug 1982, pp. 5-12

Becker, Edith and Michelle Citron, Julia Lesage, B. Ruby Rich 'Introduction to Lesbians and Film special section' *Jump Cut* no. 24-25 Mar 1981, pp. 17-21.

Martin, Donna 'Lesbianism in the Movies' *GPU News*, Wisconsin, Aug 1975, reprinted *Gay News* no. 82.

Mellen, Joan 'Lesbianism in the Movies' in *Women and Their Sexuality in the New Film,* Davis-Poynter, London, 1974.

Meyers, Janet 'Dyke Goes to the Movies' *Dyke,* New York, Spring 1976.

Millet, Bernard 'Dionysos Crucifié' *La revue du cinéma/Image et son/Ecran,* Paris, no. 353 Sept 1980, pp. 85-98.

Olson, Ray 'Affecting but too Evasive: Gay Film Work' *Jump Cut* no. 20.

Pearce, Frank 'How to Be Immoral and Ill, Pathetic and Dangerous, All at the Same Time: Mass Media and Homosexuality' in Stanley Cohen and Jock Young (eds.) *The Manufacture of the News,* Constable, London 1973, pp. 284-301.